GRADED LESSONS IN ENGLISH.

AN ELEMENTARY ENGLISH GRAMMAR,

CONSISTING OF ONE HUNDRED PRACTICAL LESSONS CAREFULLY
GRADED AND ADAPTED TO THE CLASS-ROOM.

BY

ALONZO REED, A.M.,

FORMERLY INSTRUCTOR IN ENGLISH GRAMMAR IN THE POLYTECHNIC INSTITUTE, BROOKLYN,

AND

BRAINERD KELLOGG, LL.D.,

PROFESSOR OF THE ENGLISH LANGUAGE AND LITERATURE IN THE
POLYTECHNIC INSTITUTE, BROOKLYN.

REVISED EDITION, 1901.

NEW YORK:
MAYNARD, MERRILL, & CO., PUBLISHERS.
1902.

This scarce antiquarian book is included in our special *Legacy Reprint Series*. In the interest of creating a more extensive selection of rare historical book reprints, we have chosen to reproduce this title even though it may possibly have occasional imperfections such as missing and blurred pages, missing text, poor pictures, markings, dark backgrounds and other reproduction issues beyond our control. Because this work is culturally important, we have made it available as a part of our commitment to protecting, preserving and promoting the world's literature. Thank you for your understanding.

A COMPLETE COURSE IN ENGLISH

BY

ALONZO REED, A.M., AND BRAINERD KELLOGG, LL.D.

REED'S WORD LESSONS. A Complete Speller. Designed to teach the correct spelling, pronunciation, and use of such words only as are most common in current literature, and as are most likely to be misspelled, mispronounced, or misused, and to awaken new interest in the study of synonyms and of word-analysis. 188 pages, 12mo.

REED'S INTRODUCTORY LANGUAGE WORK. A simple, varied, and pleasing, but methodical series of exercises in English to precede the study of technical grammar. 253 pages, 16mo, cloth.

REED & KELLOGG'S GRADED LESSONS IN ENGLISH. An elementary English grammar, consisting of one hundred practical lessons, carefully graded and adapted to the class room. 280 pages, 16mo, cloth.

REED & KELLOGG'S HIGHER LESSONS IN ENGLISH. A work on English grammar and composition, in which the science of the language is made tributary to the art of expression. A course of practical lessons carefully graded, and adapted to everyday use in the schoolroom. 386 pages, 16mo, cloth.

REED & KELLOGG'S HIGH SCHOOL GRAMMAR. A work dealing with the science of the English language, the history of the parts of speech, the philosophy of the changes these have undergone, and with present usage respecting forms in dispute. 285 pages, 16mo, cloth.

KELLOGG & REED'S WORD-BUILDING. Fifty lessons, combining Latin, Greek, and Anglo-Saxon roots, prefixes, and suffixes, into about fifty-five hundred common derivative words in English; with a brief history of the language. 122 pages, 16mo, cloth.

KELLOGG & REED'S THE ENGLISH LANGUAGE. A brief history of the grammatical changes of the language and its vocabulary, with exercises on synonyms, prefixes, suffixes, word-analysis, and word-building. A text-book for high schools and colleges. 220 pages, 16mo, cloth.

KELLOGG'S TEXT-BOOK ON RHETORIC. Revised and enlarged edition. Supplementing the development of the science with exhaustive practice in composition. A course of practical lessons adapted for use in high schools, academies, and lower classes of colleges. 345 pages, 12mo, cloth.

KELLOGG'S TEXT-BOOK ON ENGLISH LITERATURE. With copious extracts from the leading authors, English and American, and full instructions as to the method in which the book is to be studied. 485 pages, 12mo, cloth.

COPYRIGHT 1889, 1894, 1896 BY ALONZO REED AND BRAINERD KELLOGG;
AND 1901 BY FRANCES M. REED AND BRAINERD KELLOGG.

PREFACE.

THE plan of "Graded and Higher Lessons in English" will perhaps be better understood if we first speak of two classes of text-books with which this course is brought into competition.

Method of One Class of Text-books. — In one class are those that aim chiefly to present a course of technical grammar in the order of Orthography, Etymology, Syntax, and Prosody. These books give large space to grammatical Etymology, and demand much memorizing of definitions, rules, declensions, and conjugations, and much formal word parsing, — work of which a considerable portion is merely the invention of grammarians, and has little value in determining the pupil's use of language or in developing his reasoning faculties. This is a revival of the long-endured, unfruitful, old-time method.

Method of Another Class of Text-books. — In another class are those that present a miscellaneous collection of lessons in Composition, Spelling, Pronunciation, Sentence-analysis, Technical Grammar, and General Information, without unity or continuity. The pupil who completes these books will have gained something by practice and will have picked up some scraps of knowledge; but his information will be vague and disconnected, and he will have missed that mental training which it is the aim of a good text-book to afford. A text-book is of value just so far as it presents a clear, logical development of its subject. It must present its science or its art as a natural growth, otherwise there is no justification of its being.

The Study of the Sentence for the Proper Use of Words. — It is the plan of this course to trace with easy steps the natural development of the sentence, to consider the leading facts first and then to descend to the details. To begin with the parts of speech is to begin with details and to disregard the higher unities, without which the details are scarcely intelligible. The part of speech to which a word belongs is determined only by its function in the sentence, and inflections simply mark the offices and relations of words. Unless the pupil has been systematically trained to discover the functions and relations of words as elements of an organic whole, his knowledge of the parts of speech is of little value. It is not because he cannot conjugate the verb or decline the pronoun that he falls into such errors as "How many sounds *have* each of the vowels?" "Five years' interest *are* due." "She is older than *me*." He probably would not say "each *have*," "interest *are*," "*me* am." One thoroughly familiar with the structure of the sentence will find little trouble in using correctly the few inflectional forms in English.

The Study of the Sentence for the Laws of Discourse. — Through the study of the sentence we not only arrive at an intelligent knowledge of the parts of speech and a correct use of grammatical forms, but we discover the laws of discourse in general. In the sentence the student should find the law of unity, of continuity, of proportion, of order. All good writing consists of good sentences properly joined. Since the sentence is the foundation or unit of discourse, it is all-important that the pupil should know the sentence. He should be able to put the principal and the subordinate parts in their proper relation; he should know the exact function of every element, its relation to other elements, and its relation to the whole. He should know the sentence as the skillful engineer knows his engine, that, when there is a disorganization of parts, he may at once find the difficulty and the remedy for it.

The Study of the Sentence for the Sake of Translation. — The laws of thought being the same for all nations, the logical analysis of the sentence is the same for all languages. When a student who has acquired a knowledge of the English sentence comes to the translation of a foreign language, he finds his work greatly simplified. If in a sentence of his own language he sees only a mass of unorganized words, how much greater must be his confusion when this mass of words is in a foreign tongue! A study of the parts of speech is a far less important preparation for translation, since the declensions and conjugations in English do not conform to those of other languages. Teachers of the classics and of modern languages are beginning to appreciate these facts.

The Study of the Sentence for Discipline. — As a means of discipline nothing can compare with a training in the logical analysis of the sentence. To study thought through its outward form, the sentence, and to discover the fitness of the different parts of the expression to the parts of the thought, is to learn to think. It has been noticed that pupils thoroughly trained in the analysis and the construction of sentences come to their other studies with a decided advantage in intellectual power. These results can be obtained only by systematic and persistent work. Experienced teachers understand that a few weak lessons on the sentence at the beginning of a course and a few at the end can afford little discipline and little knowledge that will endure, and that a knowledge of the sentence cannot be gained by memorizing complicated rules and labored forms of analysis. To compel a pupil to wade through a page or two of such bewildering terms as "complex adverbial element of the second class" and "compound prepositional adjective phrase," in order to comprehend a few simple functions, is grossly unjust; it is a substitution of form for content, of words for ideas.

Subdivisions and Modifications after the Sentence. — Teachers familiar with text-books that group all grammatical instruction around the eight parts of speech, making eight independent units, will not, in the following lessons, find everything in its accustomed place. But, when it is remembered that the thread of connection unifying this work is the sentence, it will be seen that the lessons fall into their natural order of sequence. When, through the development of the sentence, all the offices of the different parts of speech are mastered, the most natural thing is to continue the work of classification and subdivide the parts of speech. The inflection of words, being distinct from their classification, makes a separate division of the work. If the chief end of grammar were to enable one to parse, we should not here depart from long-established precedent.

Sentences in Groups — Paragraphs. — In tracing the growth of the sentence from the simplest to the most complex form, each element, as it is introduced, is illustrated by a large number of detached sentences, chosen with the utmost care as to thought and expression. These compel the pupil to confine his attention to one thing till he gets it well in hand. Paragraphs from literature are then selected and are used at intervals, with questions and suggestions to enforce principles already presented, and to prepare the way informally for the regular lessons that follow. The lessons on these selections are, however, made to take a much wider scope. They lead the pupil to discover how and why sentences are grouped into paragraphs, and how paragraphs are related to each other; and they lead him on to discover whatever is most worthy of imitation in the style of the several models presented.

The Use of the Diagram. — In written analysis, the simple map, or diagram, found in the following lessons, will enable the pupil to present directly and vividly to the eye the exact function of every clause in the sentence, of every phrase in the clause, and of every word in the phrase — to picture the complete analysis of the sentence, with principal and subordinate parts in their proper relations. It is only by the aid of such a map, or picture, that the pupil can, at a single view, see the sentence as an organic whole made up of many parts performing various functions and standing in various relations. Without such a map he must labor under the disadvantage of seeing all these things by piecemeal or in succession.

But, if for any reason the teacher prefers not to use these diagrams, they may be omitted without causing the slightest break in the work. The plan of this book is in no way dependent on the use of the diagrams.

The Objections to the Diagram. — The fact that the pictorial diagram groups the parts of a sentence according to their offices and relations, and not in the order of speech, has been spoken of as a fault. It is, on the contrary, a merit, for it teaches the pupil to look through the literary order and discover the logical order. He thus learns what the literary order really is, and sees that this may be varied indefinitely, so long as the logical relations are kept clear.

The assertion that correct diagrams can be made mechanically is not borne out by the facts. It is easier to avoid precision in oral analysis than in written. The diagram drives the pupil to a most searching examination of the sentence, brings him face to face with every difficulty, and compels a decision on every point.

The Abuse of the Diagram. — Analysis by diagram often becomes so interesting and so helpful that, like other good things, it is liable to be overdone. There is danger of requiring too much written analysis. When the ordinary constructions have been made clear, diagrams should be used only for the more difficult sentences; or, if the sentences are long, only for the more difficult parts of them. In both oral and written analysis there is danger of repeating what needs no repetition. When the diagram has served its purpose, it should be dropped.

TABLE OF CONTENTS.

TWENTY-FIVE CAREFULLY GRADED STEPS IN GRAMMAR AND COMPOSITION; AND RULES FOR CAPITALIZATION AND PUNCTUATION AS NEEDED.

PAGE

1. Analysis and Composition of Sentences with Simple Subjects and Predicates — Capital Letters, Period, Interrogation Point, Parts of Speech, Nouns, Verbs, Pronouns 9–33
2. Analysis and Composition of Sentences with Subjects modified by Adjectives 33–44
3. Analysis and Composition of Sentences with Predicates modified by Adverbs 44–60
4. Analysis and Composition of Sentences with Subjects and Predicates modified by Prepositional Phrases — The Paragraph, Prepositions 60–66
5. Expansion of Adjectives and Adverbs into Phrases, and Contraction of Phrases into Adjectives and Adverbs . . 66, 67
6. Analysis and Composition of Sentences with Compound Subjects and Predicates — Conjunctions, Interjections, Exclamation Point 70–79
7. Analysis and Composition of Sentences with Nouns, Pronouns, and Adjectives as Complements — Object Complement, Attribute Complement, Narration, Position and Use of Modifiers . 79–84, 95–97
8. Analysis and Composition of Sentences with Participles and Infinitive Phrases — The Participle, Descriptive Writing 102–108
9. Analysis and Composition of Sentences with Nouns and Pronouns as Modifiers — Comma, Argument . . . 115–120
10. Analysis and Composition of Complex Sentences containing Adjective Clauses 124–128
11. Analysis and Composition of Complex Sentences containing Adverb Clauses 129–132

Table of Contents.

PAGE

12. Analysis and Composition of Complex Sentences containing Noun Clauses 136–139
13. Analysis and Composition of Compound Sentences — Independent Clauses 140, 141
14. Declarative, Interrogative, Imperative, and Exclamatory Sentences 141–144
15. Expansion and Contraction — Continued 147–150
16. Classes of Nouns and Pronouns in Sentences . . . 157–160
17. Classes of Adjectives in Sentences 161, 162
18. Classes of Verbs in Sentences 162–165
19. Classes of Adverbs in Sentences 166, 167
20. Classes of Conjunctions and of Other Connectives in Sentences 167–170
21. Nouns and Pronouns with all their Modifications in Sentences 176–192
22. Adjectives and Adverbs with their one Modification in Sentences 193–197
23. Verbs with all their Modifications in Sentences . . 197–217
24. Composition of Sentences in Paragraphs and of Paragraphs in Themes . 56–60, 86–89, 108–113, 122–124, 133–136, 145, 146, 152–156, 171–174
25. Composition of Paragraphs in Letters — Summary of Rules of Syntax, Proof Marks 229–246

REVIEW OF GRADED LESSONS 247–271

ABBREVIATIONS 272

INDEX 279

A TALK ON LANGUAGE.

[The teacher is recommended to occupy the time of at least two or three recitations, in talking with his pupils about language, always remembering that, in order to secure the interest of his class, he must allow his pupils to take an active part in the exercise. The teacher should guide the thought of his class; but, if he attempts to do all the talking, he will find, when he concludes, that he has been left to do all the thinking.

We give below a few hints in conducting this talk on language, but the teacher is not expected to confine himself to them. He will, of course, be compelled, in some instances, to resort to various devices in order to obtain from the pupils answers equivalent to those here suggested.

LESSON 1.

Teacher. — I will pronounce these three sounds very slowly and distinctly, thus: *b-u-d*. Notice, it is the power, or sound, of the letter, and not its name, that I give. What did you hear?

Pupil. — I heard three sounds.

T. — Give them. I will write on the board, so that you can see them. three letters — *b-u-d*. Are these letters, taken separately, signs to you of anything?

P. — Yes, they are signs to me of the three sounds that I have just heard.

T. — What then do these letters, taken separately, picture to your eye?

P. — They picture the sounds that came to my ear.

T. — Letters then are the signs of what?

P. — Letters are the signs of sounds.

T. — I will pronounce the same sounds rapidly, uniting them more closely — *bud*. These sounds, so united, form a spoken word. Of what do you think when you hear the word *bud?*

P. — I think of a little round thing that grows to be a leafy branch or a flower.

T. — Did you see the thing when you were thinking of it?

P. — No.

T. — Then you must have had a picture of it in your mind. We call this **mental picture** an **idea**. What called up this idea?

P. — It was called up by the word *bud*, which I heard.

T. — A spoken word then is the sign of what?

P. — A spoken word is the sign of an idea.

T. — I will call up the same idea in another way. I will write three letters and unite them thus: *bud*. What do you see?

P. — I see the word *bud*.

T. — If we call the other word *bud* a spoken word, what shall we call this?

P. — This is a written word.

T. — If they stand for the same idea, how do they differ?

P. — I see this, and I heard that.

T. — You will observe that we have called attention to four different things; viz., the **real bud**; your mental picture of the bud, which we have called an **idea**; and the **two words**, which we have called signs of this idea, the one addressed to the ear, and the other to the eye.

If the pupil be brought to see these distinctions, it may aid him to observe more closely and express himself more clearly.

A Talk on Language.

LESSON 2.

Teacher. — What did you learn in the previous Lesson?

Pupil. — I learned that a spoken word is composed of certain sounds; that a written word is composed of letters; that letters are signs of sounds; and that spoken and written words are the signs of ideas.

This question should be passed from one pupil to another till all of these answers are elicited.

All the written words in all the English books ever made are formed of twenty-six letters, representing about forty-four sounds. These letters and these sounds make up what is called verbal language.

Of these twenty-six letters, a, e, i, o, u, and sometimes w and y, are called **vowels**, and the remainder are called **consonants**.

In order that you may understand what kind of sounds the vowels stand for, and what kinds the consonants represent, I will tell you something about the human voice.

The air breathed out from your lungs beats against two flat muscles, stretched like strings across the top of the windpipe, and causes them to vibrate. This vibration makes sound. Put one end of a thread between your teeth, hold the other end of it in your fingers, draw it tight and strike it, and you will understand how voice is made. If the voice thus produced comes out through the open mouth, a class of sounds is formed which we call vowel sounds.

But, if the voice is held back by your palate, tongue, teeth, or lips, one kind of consonant sounds[1] is made. If the breath is driven out without voice, and is held back by these same parts of the mouth, the other kind of consonant sounds[1] is formed.

---

[1] Called respectively **sonants** and **surds**. We suggest that you have the pupils give the sounds of the vowel **a** in *ale, care, am, arm, ask,* and

The teacher and pupils should practice on these sounds till the three kinds can easily be distinguished.

You are now prepared to understand what I mean when I say that the **vowels** are the letters which stand for the **open sounds of the voice**, and that the **consonants** are the letters which stand for the sounds made by the **obstructed voice** and the **obstructed breath**.

The teacher can here profitably spend a few minutes in showing how ideas may be communicated by Natural Language, the language of sighs, groans, gestures of the hands, attitudes of the body, expressions of the face, tones of the voice, etc. He can show that, in conversation, we sometimes couple this Natural Language of tone and gesture with our language of words in order to make a stronger impression. Let the pupil be told that, if the passage contain feeling, he should do the same in Reading and Declaiming.

Let the following definitions be learned, and given at the next recitation.

DEFINITION. — Verbal language, or **language proper**, consists of the spoken and written words used to communicate ideas and thoughts.

DEFINITION. — **English grammar** is the science which teaches the forms, uses, and relations of the words of the English language.

---

all; the sounds of **e** in *ye, end,* and *fern;* of **i** in *ice* and *ill;* of **o** in *old, orb,* and *odd;* and of **u** in *use, rude, full, up,* and *urn.* The sounds of the sonants **b, d, g** in *gin,* **g** in *get,* **j, l, m, n, r, s** in *is,* **s** in *vision,* **v, x** in *Xenophon,* **x** in *exact,* **z** in *zero,* and **z** in *seizure;* and the sounds of the surds, **c** in *cent,* **c** in *cat* **f, h, k, p, q, s, s** in *sure,* **t,** and **x** in *wax.*

LESSON 3.

Let the pupils be required to tell what they learned in the previous Lessons.

Teacher. — When I pronounce the two words *star* and *bud*, thus: *star bud,* how many ideas, or mental pictures, do I call up to you?

Pupil. — Two.

T. — Do you see any connection between these ideas?

P. — No.

T. — When I utter the two words *bud* and *swelling* thus: *bud swelling,* do you see any connection in the ideas they stand for?

P. — Yes, I imagine that I see a bud expanding, or growing larger.

T. — I will connect two words more closely, so as to express a thought: "*Buds swell.*" A thought has been formed in my mind when I say, "*Buds swell*"; and these two words, by which something is said of something else, express that thought, and make what we call a sentence. In the former expression, *bud swelling,* it is assumed, or taken for granted, that buds perform the act; in the latter, the swelling is asserted as a fact.

Leaves falling. Do these two words express two ideas merely associated, or do they express a thought?

P. — They express ideas merely associated.

T. — "*Leaves fall.*" What do these two words express?

P. — A thought.

T. — Why?

P. — Because, in these words, there is something said or asserted of leaves.

T. — When I say, "*Falling leaves rustle,*" does *falling* tell what is thought of leaves?

P. — No.

T. — What does *falling* do?
P. — It tells the kind of leaves you are thinking and speaking of.
T. — What word does tell what is thought of leaves?
P. — *Rustle.*
T. — You see then that in the thought there are two parts; something of which we think, and that which we think about it.

Let the pupils give other examples.

LESSON 4.

Commit to memory all definitions.

DEFINITION. — A **Sentence**[1] is the expression of a thought in words.

Which of the following expressions contain words that have no connection, which contain words merely associated, and which are sentences?

1. Flowers bloom.
2. Ice melts.
3. Bloom ice.
4. Grass grows.
5. Brooks babble.
6. Babbling brooks.
7. Grass soar.
8. Doors open.
9. Open doors.
10. Cows graze.
11. Curling smoke.
12. Sugar graze.
13. Dew sparkles.
14. Hissing serpents.
15. Smoke curls.
16. Serpents hiss.
17. Smoke curling.
18. Serpents sparkles.
19. Melting babble.
20. Eagles soar.
21. Birds chirping.
22. Bird are chirping.
23. Birds chirp.
24. Gentle cows.
25. Eagles are soaring.
26. Bees ice.
27. Working bees.
28. Bees work.
29. Crawling serpents.
30. Landscape piano.
31. Serpents crawl.
32. Eagles clock.
33. Serpents crawling.

---

[1] Or, if preferred, A Sentence is a group of words expressing a thought.

LESSON 5.

REVIEW QUESTIONS.

Illustrate, by the use of **a, b,** and **p,** the difference between the sounds of letters and their names. Letters are the signs of what? What is an idea? A spoken word is the sign of what? A written word is the sign of what? How do they differ? To what four different things did we call attention in Lesson 1?

How is voice made? How are vowel sounds made? How are the two kinds of consonant sounds made? What are vowels? Name them. What are consonants? What is language proper? What do you understand by natural language? What is English grammar?

What three kinds of expressions are spoken of in Lessons 3 and 4? Give examples of each. What is a sentence?

LESSON 6.

ANALYSIS.

On the following sentences, let the pupils be exercised according to the model.

Model. — *Intemperance degrades.* Why is this a sentence? Ans.— It expresses a thought. Of what is something thought? Ans.— Intemperance. Which word tells what is thought? Ans.— *Degrades.*

1. Magnets attract.
2. Horses neigh.
3. Frogs leap.
4. Cold contracts.
5. Sunbeams dance.
6. Heat expands.
7. Sunlight gleams.
8. Banners wave.
9. Grass withers.
10. Sailors climb.
11. Rabbits burrow.
12. Spring advances.

You see that in these sentences there are two parts. The parts are the **Subject** and the **Predicate**.

DEFINITION.—The **Subject of a sentence** names that of which something is thought.

DEFINITION.—The **Predicate of a sentence** tells what is thought.

DEFINITION.—The **Analysis of a sentence** is the separation of it into its parts.

Analyze, according to the model, the following sentences.

Oral Analysis.—*Stars twinkle.* (This is a sentence, because it expresses a thought. *Stars* is the subject, because it names that of which something is thought; *twinkle* is the predicate, because it tells what is thought.

To the Teacher.—After the pupils become familiar with the definitions, the "Models" may be varied, and some of the reasons may be made specific; as, "*Plants* names the things we tell about; *droop* tells what plants do," etc.

Guard against needless repetition.

1. Plants droop.
2. Books help.
3. Clouds float.
4. Exercise strengthens.
5. Rain falls.
6. Time flies.
7. Rowdies fight.
8. Bread nourishes.
9. Boats capsize.
10. Water flows.
11. Students learn.
12. Horses gallop.

LESSON 7.

ANALYSIS AND THE DIAGRAM.

Hints for Oral Instruction.—I will draw on the board a heavy, or shaded, line, and divide it into two parts, thus:

Analysis and the Diagram. 17

We will consider the first part as the sign of the subject of a sentence, and the second part as the sign of the predicate of a sentence.

Now, if I write a word over the first line, thus — you will understand that that word is the subject of a sentence. If I write a word over the second line, thus — you will understand that that word is the predicate of a sentence.

Planets | *revolve.*

The class can see by this that "*Planets revolve*" is a sentence, that *planets* is the subject, and that *revolve* is the predicate.

Such pictures, made up of straight lines, we call **Diagrams**.

DEFINITION.— A **Diagram** is a picture of the offices and relations of the different parts of a sentence.

Analyze and diagram the following sentences: —

1. Waves dash.
2. Kings reign.
3. Fruit ripens.
4. Stars shine.
5. Steel tarnishes.
6. Insects buzz.
7. Paul preached.
8. Poets sing.
9. Nero fiddled.
10. Larks sing.
11. Water ripples.
12. Lambs frisk.
13. Lions roar.
14. Tigers growl.
15. Breezes sigh.
16. Carthage fell.
17. Morning dawns.
18. Showers descended.
19. Diamonds sparkle.
20. Alexander conquered.
21. Jupiter thunders.
22. Columbus sailed.
23. Grammarians differ.
24. Cornwallis surrendered.

In Lessons 6 and 7, you notice (1) that such subjects as *time*, *Nero*, and *morning*, each denoting only one person or thing, do not add the s-ending; and (2) that the predicates of such subjects do add it. Such subjects as *books*, *kings*, and *lions*, (3) each denoting more than one, add the s-ending; and (4) the predicates of such subjects do not add it.

This use of the simple form of the predicate with the s-form of the subject, and of the s-form of the predicate with the simple form of the subject, is called the **agreement** of the predicate with its subject.

Note, however, that, as in 7, 16, and 22 above, the s-form of the predicate is not used in telling what a person or thing did — only in telling what it does now.

LESSON 8.

COMPOSITION.

You have now learned to analyze sentences, that is, to separate them into their parts. You must next learn to put these parts together, that is, to build sentences. If the separation of a sentence into its parts is **analysis**, the putting of its parts together is **synthesis, construction,** or **composition**.

We will find one part, and you must find the other and do the building.

To the Teacher. — Let some of the pupils write their sentences on the board while others are reading theirs. Then let the work on the board be corrected.

Composition.

Correct any expression that does not make good sense, or that asserts something not strictly true; for the pupil should early be taught to think accurately, as well as to write and speak grammatically.

Correct all mistakes in spelling, and in the use of capital letters and the period.

Insist on neatness. Collect the papers before the recitation closes.

CAPITAL LETTER — RULE. — The first word of every sentence must begin with a **capital letter**.

PERIOD — RULE. — A **period** must be placed after every sentence that simply affirms, denies, or expresses a command.

Construct sentences by supplying a subject to each of the following predicates: —

Ask yourself the question, What swim, sink, hunt, etc.? The proper answers will be the subjects required.

1. —— swim.   7. —— climb. 13. —— flashes.   19. —— expand.
2. —— sinks. 8. —— creep. 14. —— flutters. 20. —— jump.
3. —— hunt.   9. —— run.   15. —— paddle.   21. —— hop.
4. —— skate. 10. —— walk.   16. —— toil.   22. —— bellow.
5. —— jingle. 11. —— snort. 17. —— terrifies. 23. —— burns.
6. —— decay. 12. —— kick.   18. —— rages.   24. —— evaporates.

This exercise may profitably be extended by requiring the pupils to supply several subjects to each predicate.

Add the **s**-ending to the predicates that are without it, and make the needed change in your subjects; drop the **s**-ending from the predicates that have it, and make the needed change in your subjects.

LESSON 9.

COMPOSITION — *Continued.*

Construct sentences by supplying a predicate to each of the following subjects: —

Ask yourself the question, Artists, sailors, tides, etc. do what? The proper answers will be the predicates required.

1. Artists ——.	13. Water ——.	25. Storms ——.
2. Sailors ——.	14. Frost ——.	26. Politicians ——.
3. Tides ——.	15. Man ——.	27. Serpents ——.
4. Whales ——.	16. Blood ——.	28. Chimneys ——.
5. Gentlemen ——.	17. Kings ——.	29. Owls ——.
6. Swine ——.	18. Lilies ——.	30. Rivers ——.
7. Clouds ——.	19. Roses ——.	31. Nations ——.
8. Girls ——.	20. Wheels ——.	32. Indians ——.
9. Fruit ——.	21. Waves ——.	33. Grain ——.
10. Powder ——	22. Dew ——.	34. Rogues ——.
11. Hail ——.	23. Boys ——.	35. Rome ——.
12. Foxes ——.	24. Volcanoes ——.	36. Briers ——.

This exercise may be extended by requiring the pupils to supply several predicates to each subject.

Add or drop the s-ending, and make the needed change in the predicates that they may agree.

You cannot become too familiar with the agreement of predicate with subject, and you cannot become familiar with it too early.

LESSON 10.

REVIEW QUESTIONS.

Of what two parts does a sentence consist? What is the subject of a sentence? What is the predicate of a sentence? What is the analysis of a sentence? What is synthesis, or composition?

What is a diagram? What rule for the use of capital letters have you learned? What rule for the period?

IMPROMPTU EXERCISE.

Let the pupils "choose sides," as in a spelling match. Let the teacher select predicates from Lesson 8, and give them alternately to the pupils thus arranged. The first pupil prefixes to his word whatever suitable subjects he can think of, the teacher judging of their fitness and keeping the count. This pupil now rises and remains standing until some one else, on his side or the other, shall have prefixed to his word a greater number of apt subjects. The struggle is to see who shall be standing at the close of the match, and which side shall have furnished the greater number of subjects. The exercise may be continued with the subjects of Lesson 9. The pupils are limited to the same time — one or two minutes.

LESSON 11.

ANALYSIS.

The **predicate** sometimes contains **more than one word**. Analyze and diagram according to the model: —

Model. — *Socrates was poisoned.*

Socrates | *was poisoned*

Oral Analysis. — This is a sentence, because it expresses a thought. *Socrates* is the subject, because ——; *was poisoned* is the predicate, because[1] ——.

1. Napoleon was banished.
2. André was captured.
3. Money is circulated.
4. Columbus was imprisoned.
5. Acorns are sprouting
6. Bells are tolled.
7. Summer has come.
8. Sentences may be analyzed.
9. Clouds are reddening.
10. Air may be weighed.
11. Jehovah shall reign.
12. Corn is planted.
13. Grammarians will differ.
14. Snow is falling.
15. Leaves are rustling.
16. Children will prattle.
17. Crickets are chirping.
18. Eclipses have been foretold.
19. Storms may abate.
20. Deception may have been practiced.
21. Esau was hated.
22. Treason should have been punished.
23. Bees are humming.
24. Sodom might have been spared.

Notice that *is*, *was*, *has*, and also *does*, are used with subjects denoting but one; and that *are*, *were*, *have*, and also *do*, are used with subjects denoting more than one.

Drop the s-ending from the subjects of 5, 6, 9, 15, 17, 18, and 23, and change *are* and *have*, that predicate and subject may agree.

Exchange the subjects of 1, 2, 3, 4, 7, 12, 14, and 21, for others with s-ending, and change *was*, *is*, and *has*, that predicates may agree with subjects.

---

[1] The word *because* — suggesting a reason — should be dropped from these "Models" whenever it may lead to mere mechanical repetition. Avoid deadly routine at whatever cost.

LESSON 12.

COMPOSITION.

Prefix the little helping words in the second column to such of the more important words in the third column as with them will make complete predicates, and join these predicates to all subjects in the first column with which they will unite and make good sense.

1	2	3
Burgoyne	are	woven.
Henry Hudson	was	defeated.
Sparrows	can be	condensed.
Comets	is	inhaled.
Time	have been	worn.
Turbans	may be	slackèd.
Lime	has been	wasted.
Steam	could have been	seen.
Air	must have been	deceived.
Carpets	were	quarreling.

LESSON 13.

Point out the subject and the predicate of each sentence in Lessons 28, 31, 34.

Look first for the word that asserts, and then, by putting *who* or *what* before this predicate, the subject may easily be found.

Read aloud in the class the sentences of Lesson 11 with the helping words *is*, *was*, *may*, *are*, *should*, etc. before their subjects. Read also the first nine sentences of Lesson 31 with *does* or *did* — as the case requires — before the subjects, making the needed changes in the predicates.

The sentences thus read become **interrogative, ask** questions; and, if written, the **interrogation point** would be used. See Lesson 63.

To the Teacher. — Most violations of the rules of agreement come from a failure to recognize the relation of subject and predicate when these parts are transposed or are separated by other words. Such constructions should therefore receive special attention.

Introduce the class to the Parts of Speech before the close of this recitation. See "Hints for Oral Instruction."

LESSON 14.

CLASSES OF WORDS.

Hints for Oral Instruction. — By the assistance of the few hints here given, the ingenious teacher may render this usually dry subject interesting and attractive. By questioning the pupil as to what he has seen and heard, his interest may be excited and his curiosity awakened.

Suppose that we make an imaginary excursion to some field or grove, where we may study the habits, the plumage, and the songs of the birds.

If we attempt to make the acquaintance of every little

feathered singer we meet, we shall never get to the end of our pleasant task; but we find that some resemble one another in size, shape, color, habits, and song. We associate these together and call them sparrows.

We find others differing essentially from the sparrows, but resembling one another. These we call robins. Others, for like reasons, we call bobolinks.

We thus find that, although we cannot become acquainted with each individual bird, they all belong to a few classes, with which we may soon become familiar.

It is so with the words of our language. There are many thousands of them, and they all belong to **eight classes**, called **Parts of Speech**.

We classify birds according to their form, color, etc., but we group words into classes, called **Parts of Speech**, with respect to their use in the sentence.

We find that many words are names. These we put into one class and call them **Nouns**.

Each pupil may give the name of something in the room; the name of a distinguished person: a name that may be applied to a class of persons; the name of an animal; the name of a place; the name of a river; the name of a mountain; the name of something which we cannot see or touch, but of which we can think; as, *beauty, mind.*

Remind the pupils frequently that these names are all nouns.

NOUNS.

DEFINITION.— A **Noun** is the name of anything.

Write in columns, headed nouns, the names of domestic animals, of garden vegetables, of flowers, of trees, of articles sold in a dry-goods store, and of things that cannot be seen or touched; as, *virtue, time, life.*

Write and arrange, according to the following model, the names of things that can float, fly, walk, work, sit, or sing:—

Nouns.

Model.— Cork, Clouds, Wood, Ships, Boys } floats or float.

Such expressions as "*Cork floats*" are sentences, and the nouns *cork, ships,* etc. are the subjects. You will find that **every subject** is a **noun** or some word or words used for a noun.

Be prepared to analyze and parse the sentences which you have made. Naming the class to which a word belongs is the **first step in parsing.**

Oral Analysis.— This **is a** sentence, because ——; *cork* is the subject, because ——; *floats* is the predicate, because ——.

Parsing.— *Cork* is a noun, because it is the name of a thing— the bark of a tree.

LESSON 15.

Select and write all the nouns in the sentences given in Lessons 28, 31, 34.

Tell why they are nouns.

In writing the nouns, observe the following rule: —

CAPITAL LETTER — RULE. — Every **proper** or individual **name** must begin with **a capital** letter.

REVIEW QUESTIONS.

With respect to what do we classify words (Lesson 14)? What are such classes called? Can you illustrate this classification? What are all names? What is a noun? What is the first step in parsing? What is the rule for writing proper names?

LESSON 16.
VERBS.

Hints for Oral Instruction. — We introduce you now to another class of words. You have learned that one very large class consists of names of things. There is another very important class used to tell what these things do, or used to express their existence.

When I say, "Plants *grow*," is *grow* the name of anything? **P.** — No. **T.** — What does it do? **P.** — It tells what plants do. It expresses action.

T. — When I say, "God *is*," what does *is* express? **P.** — It expresses existence, or being.

T.—When I say, "George *sleeps*," *sleeps* expresses being and something more; it tells the condition, or state, in which George is, or exists, that is, it expresses state of being.

All the words that assert action, being, or state of being we call **Verbs**.

Let the teacher write nouns on the board, and require the pupils to give all the words of which they can think, telling what the things named can do. They may be arranged thus:—

Noun. *Verbs.*

Plants { grow, droop, decay, flourish, revive.

Each pupil may give a verb that expresses an action of the body; as, *weep, sing;* an action of the mind; as, *study, love;* one that expresses being or state of being.

DEFINITION.—A **Verb** is a word that asserts action, being, or state of being.

The office of the verb in all its forms except two (the participle and the infinitive, see Lessons 48 and 49) is to **assert**. This it does whether the sentence affirms, denies, or asks a question.

To the Teacher.—In the exercises of this and the next two Lessons, let the pupils note the agreement of the verb with its subject.

Supply to each of the following nouns as many appropriate verbs as you can think of. Let some express being or state of being:—

Verbs.

Water ——.   Wind ——.   Pens ——.   Parrots ——.
Vines ——.   Farmers ——.   Trees ——.   Ministers ——.

One verb may consist of two, three, or four words; as, *is singing, will be sung, might have been sung*.

Form verbs by combining the words in columns 2 and 3, and add these verbs to all the nouns in column 1 with which they appropriately combine: —

1	2	3
Laws	has been	published.
Clouds	have been	paid.
Food	will be	restored.
Health	should have been	preserved.
Taxes	may be	collected.
Books	are	obeyed.

The examples you have written are sentences; **the nouns are subjects, and the verbs are predicates.**

As verbs are the only words that assert, **every predicate must be a verb** or must contain a verb.

Analyze and parse five of the sentences you have written.

Model.—*Laws are obeyed.* Diagram and analyze as in Lesson 11.

Parsing.—*Laws* is a noun, because ——; *are obeyed* is a verb, because it asserts action.

LESSON 17.

Select and write all the verbs in the sentences given in Lessons 28, 31, 34, and tell why they are verbs.

LESSON 18.

COMPOSITION.

Out of the following nouns and verbs, build as many sentences as possible, taking care that every one makes good sense and expresses a truth: —

Poems, was conquered, lambs, rebellion, stars, forests, shone, were seen, were written, treason, patriots, meteors, fought, were discovered, frisk, Cain, have fallen, fled, stream, have crumbled, day, ages, deer, are flickering, are bounding, gleamed, voices, lamps, rays, were heard, are gathering, time, death, friends, is coming, will come.

LESSON 19.

PRONOUNS.

Hints for Oral Instruction.—We propose to introduce you now to the third part of speech. **T.**—If I should ask who whispered, and some boy should promptly confess, what would he say? **P.**—"*I* whispered." **T.**—Would he mention his own name? **P.**—No. **T.**—What word would he use instead? **P.**—*I.*

T.—Suppose that I had spoken to that boy and had accused him of whispering, how should I have addressed him without mentioning his name? **P.**—"*You* whispered." **T.**—What word would be used instead of the name of the boy to whom I spoke? **P.**—*You.*

T.—Suppose that, without using his name, I had told

you what he did, what should I have said? P.—"*He* whispered." T.—What word would have been used instead of the name of the boy of whom I spoke? P.—*He*.

Repeat these questions, supposing the pupil to be a girl.

T.—If I should tell that boy to close his book when his book was already closed, what would he say without mentioning the word *book?* P.—"*It* is closed."

T.—If I should accuse several of you of whispering, and one should speak for himself and for those whispering with him, what would he say? P.—"*We* whispered."

T.—Suppose that a boy should inform me that all of the boys on that seat had whispered, what would he say? P.—"*They* whispered."

I, *you*, *he*, *she*, *it*, *we*, and *they* are not names, but they are used instead of names. We call such words **Pronouns**.

DEFINITION.— A **Pronoun** is a word used for a noun.

CAPITAL LETTERS—RULE.— The words **I** and **O** should be written in capital letters.

ANALYSIS AND PARSING.

Model.—*You will be rewarded.*

Oral Analysis.— This is a sentence, because ———; *you* is the subject, because ———; *will be rewarded* is the predicate, because ———.

Parsing.—*You* is a pronoun, because it stands for the name of the person spoken to; *will be rewarded* is a verb, because ———.

Analyze these sentences, and parse the words: —

1. We think.
2. She prattles.
3. We have recited.
4. I study.
5. You have been seen.
6. It has been decided.
7. He was punished.
8. They are conquered.
9. Thou art adored.

You see that, without changing the verb-form, *I*, *you*, and *they* may take the place of *we* in 1 and 3 above; that *you*, *we*, and *they* may take the place of *I* in 4; that *I*, *we*, and *they* may take the place of *you* in 5; and that *I*, *we*, and *you* may take the place of *they* in such a sentence as "They *have* or *had* conquered." In other words, the pronouns *I*, *we*, *you*, and *they* require the same verb-form.

An exception is *I* with *are* and *were* — forms of the verb *be*. We may say, "*We*, *you*, and *they* are or were conquered"; but, using *I*, we must say, "I *am* or *was* conquered."

Thou, as in 9, is rare; *you* takes its place. *You* may mean one or more than one, but the verb always agrees with it as if it meant more than one.

He, *she*, and *it* require *is* and *was* and the s-form of the verb seen above in *has* and *prattles*. *I* cannot be the subject of *is* or of an s-form.

To the Teacher.—Over and again, till the ear is accustomed to the right sound, have your pupils repeat aloud *I* with the agreeing verb-forms *am* and *was; we, you,* and *they* with *are* and *were; I, we, you,* and *they* with the simple verb-forms *have, go, think, study, come,* etc.; and *he, she,* and *it* with *is, was,* and the s-forms *has, thinks, goes,* *studies*, etc. Guard the pupils especially against the common errors of *was* for *were*, and *don't* for *doesn't*.

Compose nine similar sentences, using a pronoun for the subject of each, and diagram them.

To the Teacher.—Before this recitation closes, explain "Modified Subject." See "Hints for Oral Instruction."

LESSON 20.
MODIFIED SUBJECT.

Hints for Oral Instruction.—You have already learned that a noun or pronoun and a verb sometimes make a complete sentence; but we are about to show you that they are often used as the foundation only of a sentence, which is completed by adding other parts.

I hold in my hand several pieces of metal, with letters and other characters stamped on them. What do you say I have in my hand? P.—Money. T.—Yes. What other word can you use? P.—*Coin*. T.—Yes. I will write on the board this sentence: "*Coin* is stamped."

Coin is a general or class name for all such pieces of metal. I will write the word *the* before this sentence: "*The coin* is stamped." I have now made an assertion about one particular coin, so the meaning of the subject is limited by joining the word *the*.

I can limit the meaning of the subject by putting the word *a* before it. The assertion is now about one coin, but no particular one. I point to the piece near me and say, "*This coin* is stamped." I point to the one farther from me and say, "*That coin* is stamped."

When words are joined to the subject to limit its meaning, we say that the subject is modified.

The words *the*, *a*, *this*, and *that* modify the subject by limiting the word to one coin, or to one particular coin.

We can modify the subject by joining some word which will tell what kind of coin is meant.

Here is a coin dated 19—. We can say, "*The new coin is stamped.*" Here the word *new* tells what kind of coin is meant. What other words can I use to modify *coin?* P. — *Beautiful, bright, round, silver*. T. — These words *beautiful, bright, round,* and *silver* modify the subject by telling the qualities of the coin.

We call the words *the, beautiful,* etc. **Modifiers**.

DEFINITION. — A **Modifier** is a word or group of words joined to some part of the sentence to qualify or limit the meaning.

The **Subject** with its **Modifiers** is called the **Modified Subject**.

ANALYSIS.

Analyze and diagram the following sentences: —

Model. — *The genial summer days have come.*

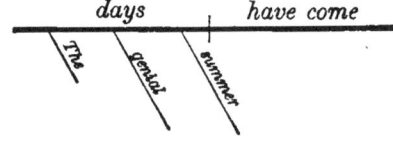

Modified Subject.

Explanation of the Diagram. — The lighter lines, joined to the subject line, stand for the modifiers, the less important parts.

Oral Analysis. — This is a sentence, because ———; *days* is the subject, because ———; *have come* is the predicate, because ———; *The, genial,* and *summer* are modifiers of the subject, because they are words joined to the subject to modify its meaning. *The genial summer days* is the modified subject.

To the Teacher. — To excite thought and guard against mere routine, pupils may, so far as they are able, make the reasons specific. For example, "*The* points out some particular clouds, *dark* tells their color," etc.

Here and elsewhere the teacher must determine how far it is profitable to follow "Models." There is great danger of wasting time in repeating forms that require no mental effort.

1. The angry wind is howling.
2. The dead leaves fall.
3. The dark clouds lower.
4. The tall elm bends.
5. All men must die.
6. The lusty bellows roared.
7. A boding silence reigned.
8. Little Arthur was murdered.
9. The mighty oak was uprooted.
10. The fragile violet was crushed.
11. The beautiful marble statue was carved.
12. The turbid torrent roared.
13. The affrighted shepherds fled.
14. The vivid lightning flashes.
15. Those elegant Etruscan vases are broken.

Change the place of certain words in 1, 5, 8, 9, 10, 11, and 15, and read these sentences as questions — see Lesson

13. Select from *do, did,* and *does* — forms of *do* — and read 4 and 14 as questions; do the same with 2 and 3; and with 6, 7, 12, and 13.

REVIEW QUESTIONS.

What is a verb? Give examples of verbs of action. Of being. Of state of being. Of how many words may a verb consist? Illustrate. Verbs are the only words that do what? What must every predicate contain?

What parts of speech are explained in the preceding Lessons? Give the definition of a pronoun. Give the rule for writing the words *I* and *O*.

Which one of these forms of the verb *be* — *am, art, is, was, are,* and *were* — is used with *I* only? Which with *I, he, she,* and *it?* In assertions of fact, like those thus far seen, what four forms of *be* is *I* not the subject of? (*Were* in certain uses, as we shall hereafter see, may be used with *I, he, she, it,* and nouns naming but one.) What forms of *be* can *he, she, it,* and nouns naming but one never be the subject of? Only what forms of *be* may *we, you, they,* and nouns naming more than one be the subject of? Which only of these forms of *have* — *has, hast, have,* and *had* — may *I* be the subject of? *He, she, it,* and nouns naming but one, be the subject of? *We, you, they,* and nouns naming more than one, be the subject of? Not classing *is* and *was* as s-forms, since the s in each is part of the root, which of the pronouns may be subjects of the s-form of verbs? Which class of nouns — those naming one, or those naming more than one — may be subjects of the s-form? What is said of *thou?* What then may you say of *art* and *hast,* above, which agree with *thou?* Of the verb-form of which *you* is the subject? What two very common errors in the use of verb-forms? How only can we guard against such errors and secure agreement of the verb with its subject?

What is the foundation on which every sentence is built? May the subject be modified? What is a modifier? What is the modified subject? Illustrate both.

LESSON 21.

COMPOSITION.

We have here prepared the foundations of sentences which you are to complete by prefixing two or more suitable modifiers to each subject. Choose and arrange your modifiers so as to make neat. truthful, and sensible assertions.

Model. —————— eminence was reached.
That lofty eminence was reached.

1. —— speaker was applauded.
2. —— difficulties were overcome.
3. —— leaf trembles.
4. —— accident happened.
5. —— books should be read.
6. —— houses are built.
7. —— soldiers perished.
8. —— opinions prevailed.
9. —— leader fell.
10. —— task is completed.

For other subjects and predicates, the teacher is referred to Lessons 7 and 11.

Build sentences by prefixing modified subjects to the following predicates : —

1. —— frolic.
2. —— crawl.
3. —— are dashing.
4. —— was caught.
5. —— escaped.
6. —— chatter.
7. —— flourished.
8. —— whistles.

Build, on each of the following subjects, three sentences similar to those in the model: —

        Model. ———— sun ————.
        The bright sun *is shining.*
        The glorious sun *has risen.*
        The unclouded sun *is sinking.*

1. —— snow ——.   2. —— dew ——.   3. —— wind ——.
        4. —— landscape ——.

To the Teacher. — Please notice that the next Lesson begins with "Hints for Oral Instruction."

LESSON 22.

ADJECTIVES.

Hints for Oral Instruction. — You are now prepared to consider the fourth part of speech. The words that are added to the subject to modify its meaning are called **Adjectives.** In succeeding Lessons you will see that adjectives may be joined to nouns that are used otherwise than as subjects of sentences.

Some grammarians have formed a separate class of the little words *the*, and *an* or *a*, calling them **Articles;** but they may be classed as adjectives, for they are joined to nouns to modify their meaning.

I will write the word *boys* on the board, and you may name adjectives that will appropriately modify it. As

Adjectives.

you give them, I will write these adjectives in a column, thus:—

Adjectives.

small		
large		
white		What words here modify *boys* by adding
black		the idea of size? What by adding the idea
straight	} boys.	of color? What by adding the idea of form?
crooked		What by adding the idea of number?
five		What are such words called? Why?
some		
all		

Let the teacher name familiar objects and require the pupils to join appropriate adjectives to the names till their stock is exhausted.

DEFINITION.— An **Adjective** is a word used to modify a noun or a pronoun.

ANALYSIS AND PARSING.

Model.—*A fearful storm was raging.* Diagram and analyze as in Lesson 20.

Written Parsing.

Nouns.	*Pronouns.*	*Adjectives.*	*Verbs.*
storm	——	A	was raging
		fearful	

Oral Parsing.—*A* is an adjective, because it is joined to the noun *storm* to modify its meaning; *fearful* is an adjective, because ——; *storm* is a noun, because ——; *was raging* is a verb, because ——.

Analyze and diagram these sentences: —

1. The rosy morn advances.
2. The humble boon was obtained.
3. An unyielding firmness was displayed.
4. The whole earth smiles.
5. Several subsequent voyages were made.
6. That burly mastiff must be secured.
7. The slender greyhound was released.
8. The cold November rain is falling.
9. That valuable English watch has been sold.
10. I alone have escaped.
11. Both positions can be defended.
12. All such discussions should have been avoided.
13. That dilapidated old wooden building has fallen.

What adjectives in these sentences modify by expressing quality? What ones modify by pointing out? What ones, by numbering?

LESSON 23.

COMPOSITION.

Prefix five adjectives to each of the following nouns: —

Shrubs, wilderness, beggar, cattle, cloud.

Write ten sentences with modified subjects, using in each two or more of the following adjectives: —

A, an, the, heroic, one, all, many, every, either, first, tenth, frugal, great, good, wise, honest, immense, square, circular, oblong, oval, mild, virtuous, universal, sweet, careless, fragrant.

Write five sentences with modified subjects, each of which shall contain one of the following words as subject:—

Chimney, hay, coach, robber, horizon.

Our knowledge of things is principally a knowledge of their qualities. A writer's style is largely affected by his choice and use of adjectives denoting these. We group a few denoting qualities perceived by the several senses. Join appropriate nouns to these:—

Seeing.

| scarlet | dingy | gaudy |
| crimson | vivid | transparent |

Hearing.

| audible | deafening | discordant |
| loud | husky | melodious |

Smelling.

| fragrant | odorous | aromatic |

Tasting.

| acid | delicious | palatable |
| pungent | insipid | luscious |

Feeling.

| rough | hard | tepid |
| dry | cold | hot |

It would be easy to add to these, especially to the first and the last class. Do so. Give some adjectives that denote intellectual qualities; some that denote moral qualities — pertaining to right and wrong.

An and *a* are forms of a word once spelled *an* and meaning one. After losing something of this force, *an* was still used before vowels and consonants alike; as, *an eagle, an ball, an hair, an use.* For the sake of ease in speaking, the word came later to have the two forms given above; *an* was retained before letters having vowel sounds, but dropped *n* and became *a* before letters having consonant sounds. This is the present usage.

Correct these errors: —

A apple; a obedient child; an brickbat; an busy boy.

Correct these errors: —

A heir; a hour; a honor.

Notice that the first letter of these words is silent.

Correct these errors: —

An unit; an utensil; an university; an ewe; an ewer; an union; an use; an history; an one-horse sled.

Unit begins with the sound of the consonant *y;* and *one*, with that of *w*.

Mention qualities belonging to each thing here named:—

   chalk   ice   brooks   clouds
   water   snow   ocean   music

Mention animals properly described by these adjectives:—

   horned   fleet   cunning   ferocious
   gentle   graceful   treacherous venomous
   faithful   useful   sagacious   ruminant

Careless persons and those with a meager list of adjectives at command overwork and abuse such words as *nice, awful, horrid, splendid, elegant, lovely,* and say *nice mountains, awful pens, horrid ink, splendid pie, elegant beef, lovely cheese,* etc.

Study the meaning of the last six adjectives, and use them to fill the following blanks:—

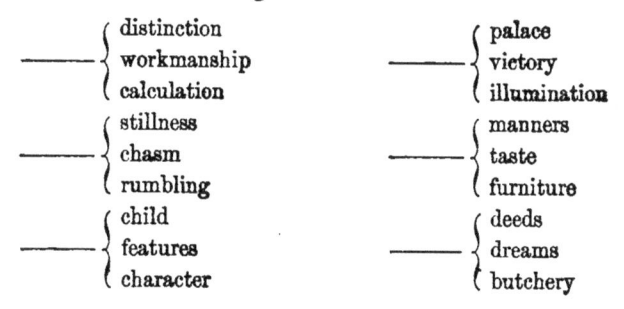

——— { distinction / workmanship / calculation }   ——— { palace / victory / illumination }

——— { stillness / chasm / rumbling }   ——— { manners / taste / furniture }

——— { child / features / character }   ——— { deeds / dreams / butchery }

This work may very profitably be extended. It begets close observation of things and care and skill in describing them.

A word picture is often spoiled by using **too many** adjectives, as: —

> A *great, large, roomy*, spacious hall;
> *Superb*, delicious, *magnificent* pumpkin-pie;
> A *stingy*, miserly, *close-fisted* fellow.

Omit those in italics, and notice how the description is improved. Subject some of your compositions to a like treatment, and note the gain.

LESSON 24.
MODIFIED PREDICATE.

Hints for Oral Instruction. — I will now show you how the predicate of a sentence may be modified.

"The ship *sails gracefully*." What word is here joined to *sails* to tell the manner of sailing? **P.** — *Gracefully*.

T. — "The ship *sails immediately*." What word is here joined to *sails* to tell the time of sailing? **P.** — *Immediately*.

T. — "The ship *sails homeward*." What word is here joined to *sails* to tell the direction of sailing? **P.** — *Homeward*.

T. — These words *gracefully*, *immediately*, and *homeward* are modifiers of the predicate. In the first sentence, *sails gracefully* is the **Modified Predicate**.

Let the following modifiers be written on the board as the pupil suggests them: —

Modified Predicate.

The ship sails { instantly. soon. daily. hither. hence. there. rapidly. smoothly. well. }

Which words indicate the time of sailing? Which, the place or direction? Which, the manner?

The teacher may suggest predicates, and require the pupils to find as many appropriate modifiers as they can.

The Predicate with its modifiers is called the **Modified Predicate.**

ANALYSIS AND PARSING.

Analyze and diagram the following sentences, and parse the nouns, pronouns, verbs, and adjectives:—

Model.— *The letters were rudely carved.*

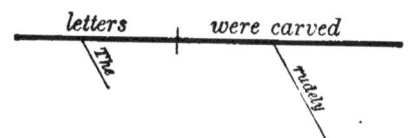

Written Parsing.— See *Model*, Lesson 22.

Oral Analysis. — This is a sentence, because —— ; *letters* is the subject, because —— ; *were carved* is the predicate, because ——; *The* is a modifier of the subject, because —— ; *rudely* is a modifier of the predicate, because —— ; *The letters* is the modified subject, *were rudely carved* is the modified predicate.

1. He spoke eloquently.
2. She chattered incessantly.
3. They searched everywhere.
4. I shall know presently.
5. The bobolink sings joyously.
6. The crowd cheered heartily.
7. A great victory was finally won.
8. Threatening clouds are moving slowly.
9. The deafening waves dash angrily.
10. These questions may be settled peaceably.
11. The wounded soldier fought bravely.
12. The ranks were quickly broken.
13. The south wind blows softly.
14. Times will surely change.
15. An hour stole on.

LESSON 25.

ANALYSIS AND PARSING.

ONE MODIFIER JOINED TO ANOTHER.

Analyze and diagram the following sentences, and parse the nouns, pronouns, adjectives, and verbs: —

Model. — *The frightened animal fled still more rapidly.*

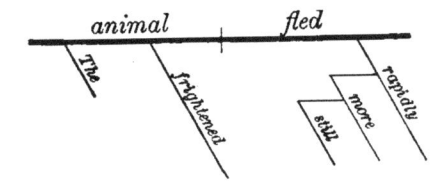

Explanation of the Diagram. — Notice that the three lines forming this group all slant the same way to show that each stands for a modifying word. The line standing for the principal word of the group is joined to the predicate line. The end of each of the other two lines is broken, and turned to touch its principal at an angle.

Oral Analysis. — This is a sentence, because ———; *animal* is the subject, because ———; *fled* is the predicate, because ———; *The* and *frightened* are modifiers of the subject, because ———; *still more rapidly* is a modifier of the predicate, because it is a group of words joined to it to limit its meaning; *rapidly* is the principal word of the group; *more* modifies *rapidly*, and *still* modifies *more*; *The frightened animal* is the modified subject; *fled still more rapidly* is the modified predicate.

1. The crocus flowers very early.
2. A violet bed is budding near.
3. The Quakers were most shamefully persecuted.
4. Perhaps he will return.
5. We laughed very heartily.
6. The yellow poplar leaves floated down.
7. The wind sighs so mournfully.
8. Few men have ever fought so stubbornly.
9. The debt will probably be paid.
10. The visitor will soon be here.
11. That humane project was quite generously sustained.
12. A perfectly innocent man was very cruelly persecuted.

REVIEW QUESTIONS.

What is an adjective? What are the words *an* or *a*, and *the* called by some grammarians? What may they be called? When is *a* used, and when *an*? Give examples of their misuse. Correct them, and give your reasons. Adjectives modify by **expressing what?**

What grows out of the careless use, or of a scanty list, of adjectives? What is said of some overworked adjectives? Of a superabundance of adjectives?

What is the modified predicate? Give an example. Give an example of one modifier joined to another.

LESSON 26.

Select your subjects from Lesson 9, and construct twenty sentences having modified subjects and modified predicates.

IMPROMPTU EXERCISE.

Select sentences from Lessons 6, 7, and 11, and conduct the exercise as directed in Lesson 10. Let the struggle be to see who can supply the greatest number of modifiers of the subject and of the predicate. The teacher can vary this exercise.

LESSON 27.

ADVERBS.

Hints for Oral Instruction. — You have learned, in the preceding Lessons, that the meaning of the predicate may be qualified by modifiers, and that one modifier may be joined to another. Words used to modify the predicate of a sentence and those used to modify modifiers belong to one class, or one part of speech, and are called **Adverbs.**

T. — " She decided *too hastily*." What word tells how she decided? P. — *Hastily*. T. — What word tells how hastily? P.— *Too.* T.— What then are the words *too* and *hastily?* P.— Adverbs.

T.— "*Too much* time has been wasted." What word modifies *much* by telling how much? P.— *Too.* T.— What part of speech is *much?* P.— An adjective. T.— What then is *too?* P.— An adverb.

T.— Why is *too* in the first sentence an adverb? Why is *too* in the second sentence an adverb? Why is *hastily* an adverb?

Let the teacher use the following and similar examples, and continue the questions: "He thinks *so;*" "*So much* time has been wasted."

Let the teacher give verbs, adjectives, and adverbs, and require the pupils to modify them by appropriate adverbs.

DEFINITION.— An **Adverb** is a word used to modify a verb, an adjective, or an adverb.

ANALYSIS AND PARSING.

Analyze, diagram, and parse the following sentences.

Model.— *We have been very agreeably disappointed.* Diagram as in Lesson 25.

For **Written Parsing,** use *Model,* Lesson 22, adding a column for adverbs.

Oral Parsing.— *We* is a pronoun, because ——; *have been disappointed* is a verb, because ——; *very* is an adverb, because it is joined to the adverb *agreeably* to tell how agreeably; *agreeably* is an adverb, because it is joined to the verb *have been disappointed* to indicate manner.

1. The plow-boy plods homeward.
2. The water gushed forth.
3. Too much time was wasted.
4. She decided too hastily.
5. You should listen more attentively.
6. More difficult sentences must be built.
7. An intensely painful operation was performed.
8. The patient suffered intensely.
9. That story was peculiarly told.
10. A peculiarly interesting story was told.
11. An extravagantly high price was paid.
12. That lady dresses extravagantly.

What adverbs in these sentences modify by expressing (1) manner, (2) degree, and (3) place or direction?

The pupil will notice that, in some of the examples above, the same adverb modifies an adjective in one sentence and an adverb in another; and that, in other examples, an adjective and a verb are modified by the same word. You learn from this why such modifiers are grouped into one class.

LESSON 28.

ANALYSIS AND PARSING.

Miscellaneous Examples for Review.

1. You must diagram neatly.
2. The sheaves are nearly gathered.
3. The wheat is duly garnered.
4. The fairies were called together.

5. The birds chirp merrily.
6. This reckless adventurer has returned.
7. The wild woods rang.
8. White, fleecy clouds are floating above.
9. Those severe laws have been repealed.
10. A republican government was established.
11. An unusually large crop had just been harvested.
12. She had been waiting quite patiently.
13. A season so extremely warm had never before been known.
14. So brave a deed[1] cannot be too warmly commended.

LESSON 29.

COMPOSITION.

MISCELLANEOUS EXERCISES FOR REVIEW.

Build sentences containing the following adverbs:—

Hurriedly, solemnly, lightly, well, how, somewhere, abroad, forever, seldom, exceedingly.

Using the following subjects and predicates as foundations, build six sentences having modified subjects and modified predicates, two of which shall contain adverbs modifying adjectives; two, adverbs modifying adverbs; and two, adverbs modifying verbs.

1. —— boat glides ——.
2. —— cloud is rising ——.
3. —— breezes are blowing ——.
4. —— elephant was captured ——.
5. —— streams flow ——.
6. —— spring has opened ——.

---

[1] *Can be commended* is the verb, and *not* is an adverb.

We here give you, in classes, the material out of which you are to build five sentences with modified subjects and modified predicates.

Select the subject and the predicate first:—

Nouns and Pronouns.	Verbs.	Adjectives.	Adverbs.
branch	was running	large, that	lustily
coach	were played	both, the	downward
they	cried	all, an	very
we	is growing	several, a	rapidly
games	cheered	amusing	not, loudly, then

LESSON 30.
ERRORS FOR CORRECTION.

Caution.—When two or more adjectives are used with a noun, care must be taken in their arrangement. If there is any difference in their relative importance, place nearest the noun the one that is most intimately connected with it.

To the Teacher.—We have in mind here those numerous cases where one adjective modifies the noun, and the second modifies the noun as limited by the first. "*All ripe apples* are picked." Here *ripe* modifies *apples*, but *all* modifies *apples* limited by *ripe*. Not all apples are picked, but only all that are ripe.

Correct the following errors of position:—

A wooden pretty bowl stood on the table.
The blue beautiful sky is cloudless.
A young industrious man was hired.
The new marble large house was sold.

Caution.—When the adjectives are of the same rank, place them where they will sound the best. This will usually be in the order of their length—the longest last.

Correct these errors:—

An entertaining and fluent speaker followed; An enthusiastic, noisy, large crowd was addressed.

Caution.—Do not use the pronoun *them* for the adjective *those*.

Correct these errors:—

Them books are nicely bound; Them two sentences should be corrected.

Pupils may be required to copy choice selections from literature, and to note carefully capitals, punctuation, and the use of adjectives, etc. We offer the following exercise as a specimen:—

> We piled with care our nightly stack
> Of wood against the chimney-back,—
> The oaken log, green, huge, and thick,
> And on its top the stout back-stick;
> The knotty fore-stick laid apart,
> And filled between with curious art
> The ragged brush; then, hovering near,
> We watched the first red blaze appear,
> Heard the sharp crackle, caught the gleam
> On whitewashed wall and sagging beam,
> Until the old, rude-furnished room
> Burst, flower-like, into rosy bloom.
> *Whittier.* — *Snow-Bound.*

Of what are the lines, above, a picture? Where and in what kind of house, do you think this picture was seen?

What object is pictured by the help of five adjectives? Are the adjectives that precede the name of this object of the same rank? Are those that follow of the same rank? What noun is modified by three adjectives of different rank? What noun by three adjectives two of which are of the same rank? What difference is found in the punctuation of these several groups? Are there any groups of words used to modify verbs or nouns? If there are and you can find them, show what words they modify.

Notice how the noun *crackle* crackles as you pronounce

it, and how the adjective *sharp* makes it penetrate. Notice how strong a picture is made in the two lines immediately before the last.

Why does Whittier use *nightly* in line 1? What does *stout* in line 4 mean? What is understood after *between* in line 6? What propriety in calling brush *ragged* in line 7? What does *sagging* in line 10 suggest? What color does *rosy* in the last line denote? Are all roses of one color?

The adjectives here used bring out the most prominent qualities of the room, and these qualities bring along with them into the imagination all the other qualities. This is what we must try to make our adjectives do.

Point out the adjectives in the selection above, and explain the office of each.

What peculiar use of capitals do you discover in these lines of poetry?

Much that has been suggested above concerning the use of adjectives will apply to adverbs also.

REVIEW QUESTIONS.

What is an adverb? Give an example of an adverb modifying an adjective; one modifying a verb; one modifying an adverb. Why are such expressions as *a wooden pretty bowl* faulty? Why is *an enthusiastic, noisy, large crowd* faulty? Why is *them books* wrong?

Thus far we have been dealing with sentences not connected with other sentences. But we seldom find them standing thus apart and alone. They are usually grouped in **paragraphs**—each sentence of the group helping to develop, and all together developing, the general thought of the paragraph. This their joint work relates them one to another, and gives them properties which they would not have if they stood alone.

To understand sentences fully then we must study them in paragraphs; to master their construction, we must compose them in paragraphs. To be known and handled as parts of a whole, the whole must be studied.

Composition of Sentences in Paragraphs.

Selection from Darwin.

Morren says that angleworms often lie for hours almost motionless close beneath the mouths of their burrows. I have occasionally noticed the same fact with worms kept in pots in the house; so that by looking down into their burrows their heads could just be seen. If the ejected earth or rubbish over the burrows be suddenly removed, the end of the worm's body may very often be seen rapidly retreating.

This habit of lying near the surface leads to their destruction to an immense extent. Every morning, during certain seasons of the year, the thrushes and blackbirds on all the lawns throughout the country draw out of their holes an astonishing number of worms; and this they could not do unless they lay close to the surface.

It is not probable that worms behave in this manner for the sake of breathing fresh air, for they can live for a long time under water. I believe that they lie near the surface for the sake of warmth, especially in the morning; and we shall hereafter find that they often coat the mouths of their burrows with leaves, apparently to prevent their bodies from coming into close contact with the cold, damp earth.

Sentences in Paragraphs.

The Uses of Words and Groups of Words. — We will break up Mr. Darwin's first group of sentences into single sentences or single statements, each having but one predicate verb.

1. Angleworms often lie for hours almost motionless close beneath the mouths of their burrows. 2. Morren says this. 3. I have occasionally noticed the same fact with worms kept in pots in the house. 4. By looking down into their burrows their heads could just be seen. 5. The ejected earth or rubbish over the burrows may suddenly be removed. 6 The end of the worm's body may then very often be seen rapidly retreating.

Find the two chief words (subject and predicate) in 1. What does *often* do? What does the group of words *for hours* do? The group *almost motionless* describes what things? The group *close beneath the mouths of their burrows*, used like a single adverb, tells what? Find the two chief words in 2. *This* helps out the meaning of *says*, but it is not an adverb. *This* is a pronoun standing here for the thing said. What whole sentence does *this* take the place of? Find the subject and the predicate verb in 3. What noun follows this verb to tell what Mr. Darwin noticed? What does *occasionally* do? What does *same* go with? What group of eight words tells in what way Mr. Darwin noticed this fact? Find the unmodified subject and predicate in 4. What does the second *their* go with? What does *by looking down into their burrows* tell? What does *just* do? In 5, put *what* before *may be removed*, and find two words either of which may be used as subject. What is the office of *the, ejected;* and the group *over the burrows?* What does *suddenly* do? Find the subject and the predicate verb in 6. *Retreating* helps out the meaning of the predicate and at the same time modifies the subject. Notice that *the end rapidly retreating* is not a sentence, nor is *worms kept in pots*, in 3. *Retreating* and *kept* here express action, but they are not predicates; they do not assert.

You learned in Lesson 16 that certain forms of the verb do not assert. *Of the worm's body* modifies what? *Then* and *very often* do what?

If you will compare these numbered sentences with Mr. Darwin's, you will see how two or more sentences are put together to make one longer sentence. You see Mr. Darwin puts our sentence 1 after *says* to tell what Morren says. What word here helps to bring two sentences together? Change this sentence about so as make *says Morren* come last. See how many other changes you can make in the arrangement of the words and groups of words in this sentence. What two words are used to join 3 and 4 together? Notice that these sentences are not joined so closely as 1 and 2, as is shown by the semicolon. Notice that *if* has much to do in joining 5 and 6. These are more closely joined than 3 and 4, but not so closely as 1 and 2. How is this shown by the punctuation? Put 5 and 6 together and change their order. Find, if you can, still another arrangement.

To the Teacher. — It is very important that pupils should learn to see words in groups and to note their offices. If difficulties and technicalities be avoided, such exercises as we suggest above may be begun very early. They will lead to an intelligent observation of language and will prepare the way for the more formal lessons of the text-book.

If time can be had, such exercises may profitably be continued through the second and third paragraphs of the selection above.

The Paragraph. — If we write about only one thing or one point, our sentences will be closely related to each other. If we write on two or more points, there will be two or more sets of sentences — the sentences of each set closely related one to another, but the sets themselves not so closely related. A group of sentences expressing what we have to say on a single point, or division, of our subject is called a **paragraph**. How many paragraphs do you find in the selection above? How are they separated on the page?

Let us examine this selection more carefully to find whether the sentences of each group are all on a single point and closely related, and whether the groups themselves are related. Do the sentences of the first paragraph all help to tell of a certain habit of angleworms? Do the sentences of the second paragraph tell what results from this habit? Do the sentences of the third paragraph tell what is thought to be the cause of this habit? If you can say *yes* to these questions, the sentences in each paragraph must be closely related. Are a habit, a result of it, and a cause of it related in thought, or meaning? If so, the paragraphs are related. In the fewest words needed, tell what this habit is, what the result of it is, and what the cause of it is.

You must now see that paragraphing helps the writer in planning his production and arranging his matter, and helps the reader to understand what the writer has done.

The Style. — We shall not here say much about what we may call the style of the author — his way of putting his thought, or manner of expressing it. But this you will notice: his words are few, plain, and simple; the arrangement of them is easy; and hence what is said is said clearly. You are nowhere in doubt about his meaning unless it be in the second paragraph. It may puzzle you to see what *their, they,* and *they* in the second sentence of this paragraph stand for. Transpose *an astonishing number of worms* and *out of their holes,* and substitute *birds* and *worms* for *they* and *they,* and see whether the meaning would not be clearer. Clearness is worth all it costs. You cannot take too much pains to be understood.

First-hand Knowledge. — As you know, we get our knowledge in two ways. We get it by seeing, and thinking about what we see; and we get it by listening to other people and reading what they have written. What we get by seeing, by observation, is first-hand knowledge; what we get from others is second-hand knowledge.

Both kinds are useful; we cannot have too much of either. But the kind that it does us most good to get and is worth most to us when got is first-hand knowledge. This especially is the kind which you should make your compositions of. In the first two paragraphs of the selection above, Darwin is telling what he saw, and in the third he is explaining what he saw. That is why what he says is so fresh and interesting.

And just one thing more. If such a man as Charles Darwin thought it worth his while to spend much time in studying and experimenting upon angleworms and then to write a large book about them, surely you need not think anything in nature beneath your notice.

ORIGINAL COMPOSITION.

In two or three short paragraphs, tell what you have observed of some worm, insect, or other creature, and what you think about it.

To the Teacher. — We suggest that what is said above be read by the pupils and discussed in the class, and that the substance of it be reproduced in the pupils' own language. Such reproduction will serve as a lesson in oral composition.

It may be profitable for the pupils to reproduce the selection from Darwin.

LESSON 31.

PHRASES INTRODUCED BY PREPOSITIONS.

Hints for Oral Instruction. — In Lessons 25 and 27, you learned that several words may be grouped together and used as one modifier. In the examples there given, the principal word is joined directly to the subject or to the predicate, and this word is modified by another word. In Lesson 30 and in this, groups of words are used as modifiers, but these words are not united with one another, or with the word which the group modifies, as they are in the preceding Lessons.

I will write on the board this sentence: "De Soto marched *into Florida.*"

T.—What tells where De Soto marched? P.—*Into Florida.* T.—What is the principal word of the group? P.—*Florida.* T.—Is *Florida* joined directly to the predicate, as *rapidly* was in Lesson 25? P.—No. T.—What little word comes in to unite the modifier to *marched?* P.—*Into.* T.—Does *Florida* alone, tell where he marched? P.—No. T.—Does *into* alone, tell where he marched? P.—No.

T.—These groups of related words are called **Phrases**. Let the teacher draw on the board the diagram of the sentence above.

Phrases of the form illustrated in this diagram are the most common, and they perform a very important function in our language.

Let the teacher frequently call attention to the fact that all the words of a phrase are taken together to perform one distinct office.

A phrase modifying the subject is equivalent to an adjective, and frequently may be changed into one. "The dew *of the morning* has passed away." What word may be used for the phrase, *of the morning?* P.—*Morning.* T.—Yes. "The *morning* dew has passed away."

A phrase modifying the predicate is equivalent to an adverb, and frequently may be changed into one. "We shall go *to that place.*" What word may be used for the phrase, *to that place?* **P.**—*There.* **T.**—Yes. "We shall go *there.*"

Change the phrases in these sentences:—

A citizen *of America* was insulted; We walked *toward home.*

Let the teacher write on the board the following words, and require the pupils to add to each, one or more words to complete a phrase, and then to construct a sentence in which the phrase is properly employed: *to, from, by, at, on, with, in, into, over.*

DEFINITION.—A **Phrase** is a group of words denoting related ideas but not expressing a thought.

ANALYSIS AND PARSING.

Analyze the following sentences, and parse the nouns, pronouns, adjectives, verbs, and adverbs.

Model.— *The finest trout in the lake are generally caught in the deepest water.*

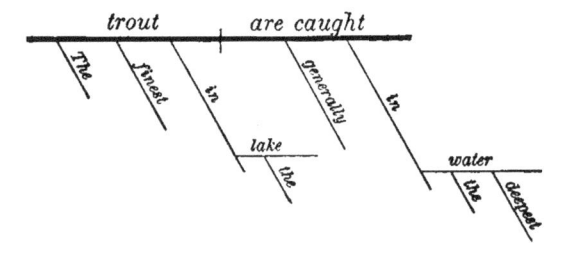

Explanation of the Diagram. — You will notice that the diagram of the phrase is made up of a slanting line standing for the introductory and connecting word, and a horizontal line representing the principal word. Under the latter are placed the little slanting lines standing for the modifiers of the principal word. Here and elsewhere all modifiers are joined to the principal words by slanting lines.

Oral Analysis. — This is a sentence, because ——; *trout* is the subject, because ——; *are caught* is the predicate, because ——; the words *The* and *finest*, and the phrase *in the lake* are modifiers of the subject, because ——; the word *generally* and the phrase *in the deepest water* are modifiers of the predicate, because ——; *in* introduces the first phrase, and *lake* is the principal word; *in* introduces the second phrase, and *water* is the principal word; *the* and *deepest* are modifiers of *water;* *The finest trout in the lake* is the modified subject, and *are generally caught in the deepest water* is the modified predicate.

1. The gorilla lives in Africa.
2. It seldom rains in Egypt.
3. The Pilgrims landed at Plymouth.
4. The wet grass sparkled in the light.
5. The little brook ran swiftly under the bridge.
6. Burgoyne surrendered at Saratoga.
7. The steeples of the village pierced through the dense fog.
8. The gloom of winter settled down on everything.
9. A gentle breeze blows from the south.
10. The temple of Solomon was destroyed.
11. The top of the mountain is covered with snow.
12. The second Continental Congress convened at Philadelphia.

Name the phrases of place in these sentences; the verbs modified by adverbs and by phrases; the nouns modified by phrases; the sentences containing each two phrases.

LESSON 32.

COMPOSITION.

Build sentences, employing the following phrases as modifiers: —

To Europe, of oak, from Albany, at the station, through the fields, for vacation, among the Indians, of the United States.

Prefix to the following predicates subjects modified by phrases: —

—— is situated on the Thames. —— was received.
—— has arrived. —— has just been completed.
—— was destroyed by an earthquake. —— may be enjoyed.

Add to the following subjects predicates modified by phrases: —

Iron ——. The Bible ——. Paul ——.
The trees ——. Sugar ——. Strawberries ——.
Squirrels ——. Cheese ——. The mountain ——.

Write five sentences, each of which shall contain one or more phrases used as modifiers.

You have all been on picnics and know a great deal about them. You know what they are and what they are for; to what places they are excursions, who go, how they go, what is carried along, what games are played, how the feast is served and eaten, what fun and recreation and enjoyment are had, and how tired everybody gets!

Study the picture minutely; name the three features of a picnic which you think are most enjoyable, and expand

"The Children's Picnic."

these three headings, or sub-topics, into three paragraphs, which when put together make a composition.

To the Teacher. — See that the paragraphs of the composition fairly exhaust the thought of the head, or sub-topic, that they stand in proper order, and that they are composed of sentences varied in kind and length.

Allow for the individuality of your pupils in the selection and in the grouping of the matter.

LESSON 33.

COMPOSITION.

Rewrite the following sentences, changing the italicized words into equivalent phrases : —

Model. — A *golden* image was made = An image *of gold* was made.

You notice that the adjective *golden* is placed before the subject, but, when changed to a phrase, it follows the subject.

1. The book was *carefully* read.
2. The old soldiers fought *courageously*.
3. A group of children were strolling *homeward*.
4. No season of life should be spent *idly*.
5. The *English* ambassador has just arrived.
6. That *generous* act was liberally rewarded.

Rewrite the following sentences, changing phrases to adjectives or adverbs, and most of the adjectives and adverbs to phrases : —

1. A thing of beauty is a joy forever.
2. English grammar is remarkably simple.

3. In all cases vulgarisms are to be shunned.
4. The conclusions of science are sometimes only highly probable.
5. The word *demijohn* has sadly puzzled people.

Change the following adjectives and adverbs into equivalent phrases, and employ the phrases in sentences of your own: —

Wooden, penniless, eastward, somewhere, here, evening, everywhere, yonder, joyfully, wintry.

Make a sentence out of the words in each line below: —

Boat, waves, glides, the, the, over.
He, Sunday, church, goes, the, on, to.
Year, night, is dying, the, the, in.
Qualities, Charlemagne, vices, were alloyed, the, great, of, with.
Indians, America, intemperance, are thinned, the, out, of, by.

LESSON 34.

PREPOSITIONS.

Hints for Oral Instruction. — In the preceding Lessons, the little words placed before nouns and with them forming phrases belong to a class of words called **Prepositions.** You noticed that these words, which you have now learned to call prepositions, introduce phrases. The preposition shows the relation of the thing denoted by the principal word of the phrase to that of the word which the phrase modifies. It serves also to connect these words.

In the sentence, "The squirrel *ran up a tree*," what

word shows the relation of the act of running, to the tree?
Ans. *Up.*

Other words may be used to express different relations. Repeat, nine times, the sentence above given, supplying in the place of *up* each of the following prepositions: *around, behind, down, into, over, through, to, under, from.*

Let this exercise be continued, using such sentences as, "The man went *into the house;*" "The ship sailed *toward the bay.*"

DEFINITION. — A **Preposition** is a word that introduces a phrase modifier, and shows the relation, in sense, of its principal word to the word modified.

ANALYSIS AND PARSING.

Model. — *Flowers preach to us.*

For **analysis** and **diagram**, see Lesson 31.

For **written parsing**, see Lesson 22. Add the needed columns.

Oral Parsing. — *Flowers* is a noun, because ——; *preach* is a verb, because ——; *to* is a preposition, because it shows the relation, in sense, between *us* and *preach; us* is a pronoun, because it is used instead of the name of the speaker and the names of those for whom he speaks.

1. The golden lines of sunset glow.
2. A smiling landscape lay before us.
3. Columbus was born at Genoa.
4. The forces of Hannibal were routed by Scipio.
5. The capital of New York is on the Hudson.
6. The ships sail over the boisterous sea.

7. All names of the Deity should begin with capital letters.
8. Air is composed chiefly of two invisible gases.
9. The greater portion of South America lies between the tropics.
10. The laurels of the warrior must at all times be dyed in blood.
11. The first word of every entire sentence should begin with a capital letter.
12. The subject of a sentence is generally placed before the predicate.

The words and the phrases in the sentences above are in what we call their **natural order**. From any of these sentences determine the natural order (1) of subject and predicate, and (2) of the phrase and the word it modifies; from 1, 6, 7, 8, and 11, determine the natural order of (3) adjectives and the nouns they modify; and from 8, 10, 11, and 12, determine the places an adverb or a phrase may hold with respect to its verb (4) when this is made up of two or more words.

If placed out of their natural order, words and phrases are said to be **transposed**; and, as we shall see, this may involve the use of the comma.

IMPROMPTU EXERCISE.

Let the teacher write on the board a subject and a predicate that will admit of many modifiers. The pupils are to expand the sentence into as many sentences as possible, each containing one apt phrase modifier. The competition is to see who can build the most and the best sentences in a given time. The teacher gathers up the slates and reads the work aloud, or has the pupils exchange slates and read it themselves.

LESSON 35.

COMPOUND SUBJECT AND COMPOUND PREDICATE.

When two or more subjects united by a connecting word have the same predicate, they form a **Compound Subject**; and, when two or more predicates connected in like manner have the same subject, they form a **Compound Predicate.**

In the sentence, "*Birds and bees* can fly," the two words *birds* and *bees*, connected by *and*, have the same predicate; the same action is asserted of both birds and bees. In the sentence, "Leaves *fade and fall*," two assertions are made of the same things. In the first sentence, *birds* and *bees* form the compound subject; and, in the second, *fade* and *fall* form the compound predicate.

Analyze the following sentences, and parse the words: —

Models. — *Napoleon rose, reigned, and fell.*
Frogs, antelopes, and kangaroos can jump.

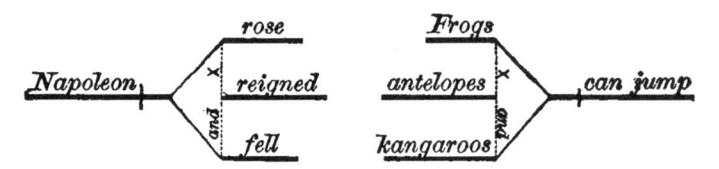

Explanation of the Diagram. — The short line following the subject line represents the entire predicate, and is supposed to be continued in the three horizontal lines that follow, each of which represents one of the parts of the compound predicate. These three lines are united by dotted lines, which stand for the connecting words. The × denotes that an *and* is understood.

Study this explanation carefully, and you will understand the other diagram.

Oral Analysis of the first sentence.

This is a sentence, because ———; *Napoleon* is the subject, because ———; *rose, reigned,* and *fell* form the compound predicate, because they belong in common to the same subject, and say something about Napoleon. *And* connects *reigned* and *fell*.

1. The Rhine and the Rhone rise in Switzerland.
2. Time and tide wait for no man.
3. Washington and Lafayette fought for American independence.
4. Wild birds shrieked, and fluttered on the ground.
5. The mob raged and roared.
6. The seasons came and went.
7. Pride, poverty, and fashion cannot live in the same house.
8. The tables of stone were cast to the ground and broken.
9. Silver or gold will be received in payment.
10. Days, months, years, and ages will circle away.

REVIEW QUESTIONS.

What is a phrase? A phrase modifying a subject is equivalent to what? Illustrate. A phrase modifying a predicate is equivalent to what? Illustrate.

What are prepositions? Give the definition. What is the natural order of subject and predicate? Of a phrase and the word it modifies? Of adjectives and their nouns? Of an adverb and the verb it modifies when this is one word? When two or more words? What do you understand by a compound subject? Illustrate. What do you understand by a compound predicate? Illustrate.

LESSON 36.

CONJUNCTIONS AND INTERJECTIONS.

The words *and* and *or*, used in the preceding Lesson to connect the nouns and the verbs, belong to a class of words called **Conjunctions**.

Conjunctions may connect words used as modifiers also, as: —

> A daring *but* foolish feat was performed.

They may connect phrases, as: —

> We shall go to Saratoga *and* to Niagara.

They may connect clauses — that is, expressions that, standing alone, would be sentences, as: —

> He must increase, *but* I must decrease.

DEFINITION. — A Conjunction is a word used to connect words, phrases, or clauses.

The **Interjection** is the eighth and last part of speech. Interjections are mere exclamations, and are without grammatical relation to any word in the sentence.

DEFINITION. — An Interjection is a word used to express strong or sudden feeling.

Examples: —

> Bravo! hurrah! pish! hush! ha, ha! alas! hail! lo! pshaw!

Conjunctions and Interjections.

Analyze the following sentences, and parse the words:—

Model.—*Hurrah! that cool and fearless fireman has rushed into the house and up the burning stairs.*

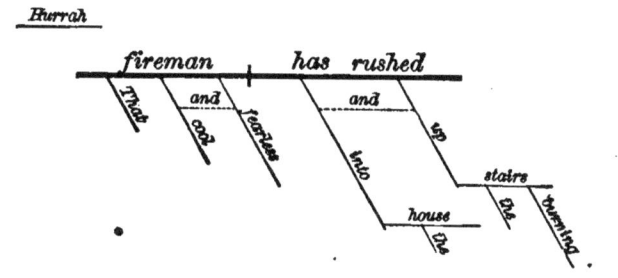

Explanation of the Diagram.—The line representing the interjection is not connected with the diagram. Notice the dotted lines, one standing for the *and* which connects the two word modifiers; the other, for the *and* connecting the two phrase modifiers.

Written Parsing.

N.	Pro.	Adj.	Vb.	Ad.	Prep.	Conj.	Int.
fireman		the	has rushed		into	and	hurrah
house		that			up	and	
stairs		cool					
		fearless					
		burning					

Oral parsing of the conjunction and the interjection.

The two *ands* are conjunctions, because they connect. The first connects two word modifiers; the second, two phrase modifiers. *Hurrah* is an interjection, because it expresses a burst of sudden feeling.

1. The small but courageous band was finally overpowered.
2. Lightning and electricity were identified by Franklin.
3. A complete success or an entire failure was anticipated.
4. Good men and bad men are found in all communities.
5. Vapors rise from the ocean and fall upon the land.
6. The Revolutionary War began at Lexington and ended at Yorktown.
7. Alas! all hope has fled.
8. Ah! I am surprised at the news.
9. Oh! we shall certainly drown.
10. Pshaw! you are dreaming.
11. Hurrah! the field is won.

Were identified in 2 is asserted of two things; *rise* and *fall* in 5, of two or more. *Was anticipated* in 3 is asserted of only one thing,—success or failure,—and *has fled* in 7, of only one.

Singular means one, **plural** means more than one, and **agreement** means that plural subjects have plural verbs, and subjects in the singular have verbs in the singular. Two or more subjects in the singular connected by *and* and naming different things make a plural subject; and two or more subjects in the singular connected by *or, nor, either . . . or, neither . . . nor* make a subject in the singular.

The adjectives *each, every,* and *no,* belonging to nouns in the singular, show that the things named are taken separately, and that the verb must be in the singular.

Remembering now that nouns with s-ending are plural

and that verbs with s-ending are singular, justify the italicized verb-forms in these sentences: —

1. Each word and gesture *was* suited to the thought.
2. In the death of Franklin, a philosopher and statesman *was* lost to the world.
3. Beauty and utility *are* combined in nature.
4. Either beauty or utility *appears* in every natural object.
5. Here *is* neither beauty nor utility.
6. Time and tide *wait* for no man.
7. Wisdom and prudence *dwell* with the lowly man.
8. *Does* either landlord or tenant profit by this bill?
9. Neither landlords nor tenants *profit* by this bill.
10. Every fly, bee, beetle, and butterfly *is* provided with six feet.
11. That desperate robber and murderer *was* finally secured.
12. Every bud, leaf, and blade of grass *rejoices* after the warm rain.
13. That desperate robber and that murderer *were* finally secured.
14. The builder and owner of the yacht *has* sailed from Liverpool.
15. The builder and the owner of the yacht *have* sailed from Liverpool.
16. A lame and blind man *was* provided with food and lodging.
17. A lame and a blind man *were* provided with food and lodging.
18. No dew, no rain, no cloud *comes* to the relief of the parched earth.

Select the sentences with subjects in the singular connected by *and*, naming (1) different things, and (2) the same thing; (3) connected by *or, nor, either . . . or, neither . . . nor;* and (4) modified by *each, every*, and *no*. Point out the effect of repeating *that, the*, or *a* in 13, 15, and 17.

1. Neither John nor his *sisters were* there.
2. *Action*, and not words, *is* needed.
3. *Bread and milk is* good food.
4. The *committee are* unable to agree on *their* report.
5. The *committee has* made *its* report.

Pupils will see, in examples like 1 above, that the verb agrees with its nearest subject, and that the plural subject is usually placed next the verb; in examples like 2, that the verb agrees with the affirmative subject, another verb being understood with the negative subject; that in 3, *bread and milk* represents one article of food; and that in 4, the individuals of the committee are thought of; while in 5, the committee as a whole is thought of. In 4 and 5, the agreement of the pronoun also may be noted. Pronouns may be introduced into many of the preceding exercises and the pupils led to apply to the agreement of the pronoun with its antecedent what has been learned of the agreement of the verb with its subject. Let the pupils determine why the following connected subjects are arranged in the proper order: —

You and I are invited.   You and Mary are invited.
Mary and I are invited.   You and Mary and I are invited.

LESSON 37.
PUNCTUATION AND CAPITAL LETTERS.

Comma — Rule. — Phrases that are placed out of their natural order and made emphatic, or that are loosely connected with the rest of the sentence, should be set off by the comma.

Punctuation and Capital Letters.

Punctuate the following sentences: —

Model. — The cable, *after many failures*, was successfully laid.

Upon the platform 'twixt eleven and twelve I'll visit you.
To me this place is endeared by many associations.
Your answers with few exceptions have been correctly given.
In English much depends on the placing of phrases.

COMMA — RULE. — **Words or phrases connected by conjunctions are separated from each other by the comma unless all the conjunctions are expressed.**

Punctuate the following sentences: —

Model. — Cæsar *came, saw, and conquered.*
Cæsar *came and saw and conquered.*
He traveled in *England, in Scotland, and in Ireland.*

Tell why the comma is used in the first and third sentences but not in the second.

A brave prudent and honorable man was chosen.
Augustus Tiberius Nero and Vespasian were Roman emperors.
Through rainy weather across a wild country over muddy roads after a long ride we came to the end of our journey.

PERIOD AND CAPITAL LETTER — RULE. — **Abbreviations generally begin with capital letters and are always followed by the period.**

Correct the following errors, and (see list at the end of the book) tell what these abbreviations stand for: —

Model. — *Mr., Esq., N.Y., P.M.*

gen, a m, mrs, no, u s a, n e, eng, p o, rev, prof, dr, gram, capt, col, co, va, conn, feb, n o, n, oct, pres, sat, vt, apr, ky, a d, gov, wed, s, w, treas, maj, sec, geo, hon.

Pick out from the list of abbreviations a score of the most common ones that do not begin with capital letters, and tell what they stand for.

Exclamation Point — Rule.—All **exclamatory expressions** must be followed by the exclamation point.

Punctuate the following expressions: —

Model. — *Ah! Oh! Zounds! Stop pinching!*

Pshaw, whew, alas, ho Tom, hallo Sir, good-by, welcome.

LESSON 38.
COMPOSITION.

Write predicates for the following compound subjects: —

Snow and hail; leaves and branches; a soldier or a sailor; London and Paris.

Write compound predicates for the following subjects: —

The sun; water; fish; steamboats; soap; farmers; fences; clothes.

Write subjects for the following compound predicates: —

Live, feel, and grow; judges and rewards; owes and pays; inhale and exhale; expand and contract; flutters and alights; fly, buzz, and sting; restrain or punish.

Write compound subjects before the following predicates: —

May be seen; roar; will be appointed; have flown; has been recommended.

Write compound predicates after the following compound subjects: —

Boys, frogs, and horses; wood, coal, and peat; Maine and New Hampshire; Concord, Lexington, and Bunker Hill; pins, tacks, and needles.

Write compound subjects before the following compound predicates: —

Throb and ache; were tried, condemned, and hanged; eat, sleep, and dress.

Choose your own material and write five sentences, each having a compound subject and a compound predicate.

LESSON 39.

COMPLEMENTS.

Hints for Oral Instruction. — When we say, "The sun *gives*," we express no complete thought. The subject *sun* is complete, but the predicate *gives* does not make a complete assertion. When we say, "The sun *gives light*," we do utter a complete thought. The predicate *gives* is completed by the word *light*. Whatever fills out, or completes, we call a **Complement**. We will therefore call *light* the complement of the predicate. As *light* completes the predicate by naming the thing acted upon, we call it the Object Complement.

Expressions like the following may be written on the board, and by a series of questions the pupils may be made to dwell upon these facts till they are thoroughly understood: —

The officer arrested ——; the boy found ——;
Charles saw ——; coopers make ——.

Besides verbs requiring object complements, there are those that do not make complete sense without the aid of a complement of another kind.

A complete predicate does the asserting and expresses what is asserted. In the sentence, "Armies *march*," *march* is a complete predicate, for it does the asserting and expresses what is asserted; viz., marching. In the phrase, *armies marching*, *marching* expresses the act denoted by *march*, but it asserts nothing. In the sentence, "Chalk *is white*," *is* does the asserting, but it does not express what is asserted. We do not wish to assert merely that chalk is or exists. What we wish to assert of chalk is the quality expressed by the adjective *white*. As *white* expresses a quality or attribute, we may call it an Attribute Complement.

Using expressions like the following, let the facts given above be drawn from the class by means of questions: —

Grass growing; grass grows; green grass; grass is green.

Complements.

DEFINITION.— The **Object Complement of a sentence** completes the predicate, and names that which receives the act.

DEFINITION.— The **Attribute Complement of a sentence** completes the predicate and belongs to the subject.

The complement with all its modifiers is called the **Modified Complement**.

ANALYSIS AND PARSING.

Model.— *Fulton invented the first steamboat.*

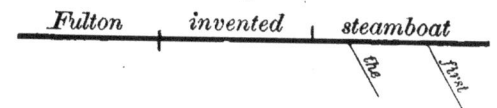

Explanation of the Diagram.— You will see that the line standing for the object complement is a continuation of the predicate line, and that the little vertical line only touches this without cutting it.

Oral Analysis.— *Fulton* and *invented*, as before. *Steamboat* is the object complement, because it completes the predicate, and names that which receives the act. *The* and *first*, as before. *The first steamboat* is the modified complement.

1. Cæsar crossed the Rubicon.
2. Morse invented the telegraph.
3. Ericsson built the Monitor.
4. Hume wrote a history.
5. Morn purples the east.
6. Antony beheaded Cicero.

Model.— *Gold is malleable.*

In this diagram, the line standing for the attribute complement, like the object line, is a continuation of the predicate line; but notice the difference in the little mark separating the incomplete[1] predicate from the complement.

Oral Analysis. — *Gold* and *is*, as before. *Malleable* is the attribute complement, because it completes the predicate, and expresses a quality belonging to gold.

7. Pure water is tasteless.
8. The hare is timid.
9. Fawns are graceful.
10. This peach is delicious.
11. He was extremely prodigal.
12. The valley of the Mississippi is very fertile.

LESSON 40.

ERRORS IN THE USE OF MODIFIERS.

Caution. — Place adverbs where there can be no doubt as to the words they modify.

Correct these errors: —

I only bring forward a few things.
Hath the Lord only[2] spoken by Moses?
We merely speak of numbers.
The Chinese chiefly live upon rice.

---

[1] Hereafter we shall call the verb the predicate; but, when followed by a complement, it must be regarded as an incomplete predicate.

[2] Adverbs sometimes modify phrases

Caution. — In placing the adverb, regard must be had to the sound of the sentence.

Correct these errors: —

>We always should do our duty.
>The times have changed surely.
>The work will be never finished.
>He must have certainly been sick.

Caution. — Adverbs must not be used for adjectives.

Correct these errors: —

>I feel badly.
>Marble feels coldly.
>She looks nicely.
>It was sold cheaply.
>It appears still more plainly.
>That sounds harshly.
>I arrived at home safely.

Caution. — Adjectives must not be used for adverbs.

Correct these errors: —

>The bells ring merry.
>The curtain hangs graceful.
>That is a decided weak point.
>Speak no coarser than usual.
>These are the words nearest connected.
>Talk slow and distinct.
>She is a remarkable pretty girl.

It is often difficult to distinguish an adjective complement from an adverb modifier. We offer the following assistance: —

"Mary arrived *safe*." As we here wish to tell the condition of Mary on her arrival, and not the manner of her arriving, we use *safe*, not *safely*. "My head feels *bad*" (is in a bad condition, as perceived by the sense of feeling). "The sun shines *bright*" (is bright — quality — as perceived by its shining).

You must determine whether you wish to tell the quality of the thing named or the manner of the action.

When the idea of **being is** prominent in the verb, as in the examples above, you **see** that the adjective, and not the adverb, follows.

Show that the following adjectives and adverbs are used correctly:—

1. I feel sad.
2. I feel deeply.
3. I feel miserable.
4. He appeared prompt and willing.
5. He appeared promptly and willingly.
6. She looks beautiful.
7. She sings beautifully.

REVIEW QUESTIONS.

What is a conjunction? What is an interjection? Give two rules for the use of the comma (Lesson 37). What is the rule for writing abbreviations? What is the rule for the exclamation point? What is an object complement? What is an attribute complement? Illustrate both. What are the cautions for the position of the adverb? What are the cautions for the use of the adverb and the adjective? Tell when we use the adjective and when we use the adverb.

Composition of Sentences and of Paragraphs.

Selection from Habberton — "Helen's Babies."

The whistles completed, I was marched with music to the place where the "Jacks" grew. It was just such a place as boys delight in — low, damp, and boggy, with a brook hidden away under overhanging ferns and grasses.

1. The children knew by sight the plant that bore the "Jacks," and every discovery was announced by a piercing shriek of delight. 2. At first I looked hurriedly toward the brook as each yell clove the air; but, as I became accustomed to it, my attention was diverted by some exquisite ferns. 3. Suddenly, however, a succession of shrieks announced that something was wrong, and across a large fern I saw a small face in a great deal of agony. 4. Budge was hurrying to the relief of his brother, and was soon as deeply embedded as Toddie was in the rich, black mud at the bottom of the brook. 5. I dashed to the rescue, stood astride the brook, and offered a hand to each boy, when a treacherous tuft of grass gave way, and, with a glorious splash, I went in myself.

This accident turned Toddie's sorrow to laughter, but I can't say I made light of my misfortune on that account. To fall into clear water is not pleasant, even when one is trout-fishing; but to be clad in white trousers and suddenly drop nearly knee-deep into the lap of mother earth is quite a different thing.

I hastily picked up the children and threw them upon the bank, and then strode off and tried to shake myself, as I have seen a Newfoundland dog do. The shake was not a success — it caused my trousers' legs to flap dismally about my ankles, and sent the streams of treacherous ooze trickling down into my shoes. My hat, of drab felt, had fallen off by the brookside, and been plentifully spattered as I got out.

"I RUSHED TO THE RESCUE."

The Uses of Words and Groups of Words. — We will put the first paragraph above into single sentences.

1. The whistles completed, we were marched with music to the place. 2. The "Jacks" grew in this place. 3. It was a place low, damp, and boggy, with a brook hidden away under overhanging ferns and grasses. 4. Boys delight in such a place.

Find the subject noun (or pronoun) and the predicate verb in each of the four sentences above. Does *the whistles completed* make complete sense? You learned in Lesson 16 that some forms of the verb do not assert — cannot be predicates. Does *brook hidden*, in 3, contain a predicate? What can you say of *hidden*? Find a noun in 3 used to complete the predicate and make the meaning of the subject plainer. What group of adjectives modifies *place*? Tell why these three adjectives are separated by commas. What long phrase describes *place*?

Find the first verb in the second paragraph of the selection. What is the object complement of this verb? *That bore the "Jacks"* does what? The pronoun *that* stands for *plant*. *The plant bore the "Jacks,"* standing by itself, is a complete sentence; but by using *that* for *plant* the whole expression is made to do the work of an adjective. What conjunction joins on another expression that by itself would make a complete sentence? What are the subject and the predicate of this added sentence? *By a piercing shriek of delight* does what? Of what use are the phrases *at first* and *toward the brook* in sentence 2? What group of words is joined to *looked* to tell on what occasion or how often? Find in this group a subject, a predicate, and an object complement. What connects this group to *looked*? What two sentences does *but* here bring together? Does the semicolon show that this connection is close? Point out what you think to be the leading subject and the leading verb after *but*. *By some exquisite ferns* is joined to what? What group of words goes with *was diverted* to tell when? Find in this group a subject, a predicate, and an attribute complement. Point out in the first part of 3 the leading subject and its verb. What does *suddenly* go with? What does *of shrieks* modify? *However* is loosely thrown in to carry the attention back to what goes before. Notice the commas. Answer the question made by putting *what* after *announced*. In this group of words used as object complement can you find a subject, a predicate, and a complement? What two sentences does *and* here bring together? Point out the subject, the predicate, and the complement in the second of these. *Across a large fern* is joined like an adverb to what? *In a great deal of agony* modifies what? Find a compound predicate in 4. What phrase is joined to *was embedded* to tell where? The group of words *as deeply as Toddie was (embedded)* is joined to what? Find in 5 a compound predicate made up of three verbs, one of which has an object complement.

To the Teacher. — See suggestions with the preceding selection. If our exercises on the second paragraph above are found too hard, the compound and complex sentences may be broken up into single statements.

The Narrative. — This selection from "Helen's Babies" is a story and therefore a narrative. But there are some descriptive touches in it. All stories must have such touches. Perhaps it is not always essential to distinguish between narration and description, but it is worth your while to do it occasionally. Try to point out the descriptive parts in these paragraphs. You certainly can find a descriptive sentence in the first paragraph, and descriptive words, phrases, and clauses throughout the selection. What help to the narrative do these descriptive touches give?

The Paragraphs. — What have you learned about the sentences that make up one paragraph? Are the paragraphs more, or less, closely related than the sentences of each paragraph? Why? Examine these paragraphs and see whether any sentences can be changed from one paragraph to another. If you think they can, give your reason. Is the order of these paragraphs the right one? Can the order anywhere be changed without throwing the story out of joint? Why?

The General Topic and the Sub-topics. — We shall find that every composition has its general subject, and that each paragraph in the composition has its own particular subject. Let us call the subject of the whole composition the **general topic**. *Sub* means *under*, and so let us call the point which each paragraph develops a **subtopic**. In the story above we may find some such outline as the following: —

AN EXCURSION IN SEARCH OF "JACKS."
1. The Place where Jacks grow.
2. The Mishap to the Excursionists.
3. The Uncle takes his Seriously.
4. His Attempt at Repairs.

Do you think that such a **framework** helps a writer to tell his story? Do you not think that each sub-topic must suggest some thoughts that the general topic alone would not suggest? If you keep clearly before you the sub-topic of your paragraph, what effect do you think it will have on the thoughts and the sentences of that paragraph? With a good framework before you, must not your story move along in an orderly way from a beginning to an end? Have you ever heard stories badly told? If so, what were the faults?

ORIGINAL COMPOSITION.

Have you not had some experience that you can work up into a good story? If you have, tell the story upon paper, making use of the instruction we have given you in our talk above.

To the Teacher. — Perhaps a reproduction of the story above may be profitable.

LESSON 41.

THE POSITION AND USE OF MODIFIERS.

Caution. — Phrase modifiers should be placed as near as may be to the words they modify.

Copy the following, and note the arrangement and the punctuation of the phrases: —

(g) This place is endeared to me by many associations.
(h) To me, this place is endeared by many associations.
(i) Your answers, with few exceptions, have been correctly given.
(j) He applied for the position, without a recommendation.

When two or more phrases belong to the same word, the one most closely modifying it stands nearest to it.

In the first sentence above, *to me* tells to whom the place is endeared; *by many associations* tells how it is endeared to me, and is therefore placed after *to me*. Try the effect of placing *to me* last. Phrases, like adjectives, may be of different rank.

Notice that *to me*, in (h) above, is transposed, and thus made emphatic, and that it is set off by the comma.

In (i), the phrase is loosely thrown in as if it were not essential, thus making a break in the sentence. To make this apparent to the eye we set the phrase off by the comma.

Place the phrase of (i) in other positions, and set it off. When the phrase is at the beginning or at the end of the sentence, how many commas do you need to set it off? How many, when it is in the middle?

Do you find any choice in the four positions of this phrase? After having been told that your answers were correct, would it be a disappointment to be told that they are not all correct? Is the interest in a story best kept up by first telling the important points and then the unimportant particulars? What then do you think of placing this phrase at the end?

What does the last phrase of (j) modify? Take out the comma, and then see whether there can be any doubt as to what the phrase modifies.

In the placing of adverbs and phrases great freedom is often allowable, and the determining of their best possible position affords an almost unlimited opportunity for the exercise of taste and judgment.

Such questions as those on (i) above may suggest a mode of easy approach to what is usually relegated to rhetoric. Let the pupils see that **phrases** may be **transposed** for various reasons — **for emphasis**, as in (h) above; for the purpose of exciting the **read**er's curiosity and **holding** his **attention** till the complete statement is made, as in (i) above, or in, "In the dead of night, with a chosen band, under the cover of a truce, he approached"; and for the sake of **balancing the sentence** by letting some of the modifying terms precede, and some follow, the principal parts; as, "In 1837, on the death of William IV., Victoria succeeded to the throne."

Pupils may note the transposed words and phrases in

the following sentences, and explain their office and the effect of the transposition: —

1. Victories, indeed, they were.
2. Down came the masts.
3. Here stands the man.
4. Doubtful seemed the battle.
5. Wide open stood the door.
6. A mighty man is he.
7. That gale I well remember.
8. Behind her rode Lalla Rookh.
9. Blood-red became the sun.
10. Louder waxed the applause.
11. Him the Almighty Power hurled headlong.
12. Slowly and sadly we laid him down.
13. Into the valley of death rode the six hundred.
14. So died the great Columbus of the skies.
15. Æneas did, from the flames of Troy, upon his shoulders, the old Anchises bear.
16. Such a heart in the breast of my people beats.
17. The great fire up the deep and wide chimney roared.
18. Ease and grace in writing are, of all the acquisitions made in school, the most difficult and valuable.

Read the following sentences in the transposed order, and explain the effect of the change: —

19. He could not avoid it.
20. He would not escape.
21. I must go.
22. He ended his tale here.
23. It stands written so.
24. She seemed young and sad.
25. I will make one more effort to save you.
26. My regrets were bitter and unavailing.
27. I came into the world helpless.
28. A sincere word was never utterly lost.
29. Catiline shall no longer plot her ruin.

ORDER OF WORDS IN QUESTIONS.

30. Who wrote the Declaration of Independence?
31. What states border on the Gulf of Mexico?
32. Whom did you see?
33. What is poetry?
34. Which course will you choose?
35. Why are the days shorter in winter?
36. When was America discovered?
37. Were you there?
38. Has the North Pole been reached?

When the interrogative word is subject or a modifier of it, is the order natural, or transposed? See 30 and 31 above.

When the interrogative word is object or attribute complement, or a modifier of either, what is the order? See 32, 33, and 34.

When the interrogative word is an adverb, what is the order? See 35 and 36.

When there is no interrogative word, what is the order? See 37 and 38.

Correct these errors: —

A fellow was arrested with short hair.
He died and went to his rest in New York.
He is to speak of the landing of the Pilgrims at the Academy of Music.
Report any inattention of the waiters to the cashier.
Some garments were made for the family of thick material.
The vessel was beautifully painted with a tall mast.

I perceived that it had been scoured with half an eye.
A house was built by a mason of brown stone.
A pearl was found by a sailor in a shell.

Punctuate these sentences when corrected.

Caution. — Care must be taken to select the right preposition. For it, consult the Unabridged Dictionaries.

Correct these errors: —

They halted with the river on their backs.
The cat jumped on the chair.
He fell onto the floor.
He went in the house.
Between each page.
He died for thirst.
This is different to that.
The choice lies among the three candidates.
I am angry at him.

Caution. — Do not use two negative, or denying, words so that one shall contradict the other, unless you wish to affirm.

Correct these errors: —

I haven't no umbrella.

Correct by dropping either the adjective *no* or the adverb *not;* as, I have *no* umbrella, or I have *not* an umbrella.

I didn't say nothing.
I can't do this in no way.

No other emperor was so wise nor powerful.
Nothing can never be annihilated.

LESSON 42.

ANALYSIS AND PARSING

1. Brutus stabbed Cæsar.
2. Man is an animal.
3. Washington captured Cornwallis.
4. Wellington defeated Napoleon at Waterloo.
5. Balboa discovered the Pacific ocean.
6. Vulcan was a blacksmith.
7. The summer has been very rainy.
8. Columbus made four voyages to the New World.
9. The moon reflects the light of the sun.
10. The first vice president of the United States was John Adams.
11. Roger Williams was the founder of Rhode Island.
12. Harvey discovered the circulation of blood.
13. Diamonds are combustible.
14. Napoleon died a prisoner, at St. Helena.
15. In 1619 the first shipload of slaves was landed at Jamestown.

The pupil will notice that *animal*, in sentence 2, is an attribute complement, though it is not an adjective expressing a quality belonging to man, but a noun denoting his class. **Nouns** then may be **attribute complements.**

The pupil will notice also that some of the object and attribute complements above have phrase modifiers.

LESSON 43.

COMPOSITION.

Using the following predicates, construct sentences having subjects, predicates, and object complements with or without modifiers : —

—— climb ——; —— hunt ——; —— command ——; —— attacked ——; —— pursued ——; —— shall receive ——; —— have seen ——; —— love ——.

Change the following expressions into sentences by asserting the qualities here assumed. Use these verbs for predicates: —

Is, were, appears, may be, became, was, have been, should have been, is becoming, are.

Model. — *Heavy* gold ; Gold *is heavy.*

Green fields ; sweet oranges ; interesting story ; brilliant sunrise ; severe punishment ; playful kittens ; warm weather ; pitiful sight ; sour grapes ; amusing anecdote.

Prefix to the following nouns several adjectives expressing assumed qualities, and then make complete sentences by asserting the same qualities : —

Model. — white ⎫
          brittle ⎬ chalk.
          soft ⎭

Chalk *is white.*
Chalk *is brittle.*
Chalk *is soft.*

Gold, pears, pens, lead, water, moon, vase, rock, lakes, summer, ocean, valley.

Find your own material, and build two sentences having object complements, and two having attribute complements.

LESSON 44.

ANALYSIS AND PARSING.

MISCELLANEOUS.

Models. —

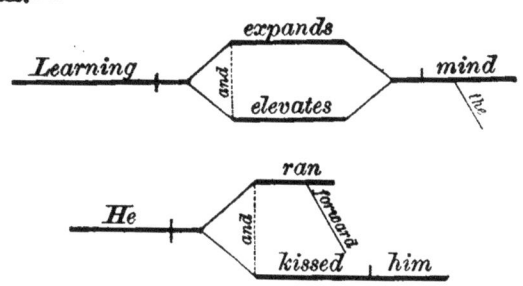

Explanation of the Diagram. — In the first diagram, the two lines standing for the two parts of the predicate are brought together, and are followed by the complement line. This shows that the two verbs are completed by the same object.

In the second diagram, one of the predicate lines is followed by a complement line; but the two predicate lines are not united, for the two verbs have not a common object.

1. Learning expands and elevates the mind.
2. He ran forward and kissed him.
3. The earth and the moon are planets.
4. The Swiss scenery is picturesque.
5. Jefferson was chosen the third president of the United States

6. Nathan Hale died a martyr to liberty.
7. The man stood speechless.
8. Labor disgraces no man.
9. Aristotle and Plato were the most distinguished philosophers of antiquity.
10. Josephus wrote a history of the Jews.
11. This man seems the leader of the whole party.
12. The attribute complement completes the predicate and belongs to the subject.
13. Lord Cornwallis became governor of Bengal after his disastrous defeat.
14. The multitude ran before him and strewed branches in the way.
15. Peter Minuits traded with the Indians, and bought the whole island of Manhattan for twenty-four dollars.

Pick out the phrases (1) of place and (2) of time in these sentences.

LESSON 45.

ANALYSIS AND PARSING.

MISCELLANEOUS.

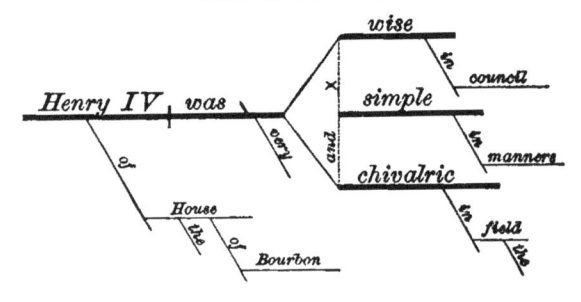

Explanation of the Diagram. — In this diagram the complement line separates into three parts, to each of which is joined a phrase diagram. The line standing for the word-modifier is joined to that part of the complement line which represents the entire attribute complement.

1. Henry IV., of the House of Bourbon, was very wise in council, simple in manners, and chivalric in the field.
2. Cæsar defeated Pompey at Pharsalia.
3. The diamond is the most valuable gem.
4. The Greeks took Troy by stratagem.
5. The submarine cable unites the continent of America and the Old World.
6. The Gauls joined the army of Hannibal.
7. Columbus crossed the Atlantic with ninety men, and landed at San Salvador.
8. Vulcan made arms for Achilles.
9. Cromwell gained at Naseby a most decisive victory over the Royalists.
10. Columbus was a native of Genoa.
11. God tempers the wind to the shorn lamb.
12. The morning hour has gold in its mouth.
13. The mill of the gods grinds late, but grinds to powder.
14. A young farmer recently bought a yoke of oxen, six cows, and a horse.
15. America has furnished to the world tobacco, the potato, and Indian corn.

Pick out the place and the manner phrases in these sentences. What phrases can you turn into adjectives or adverbs, and what adjectives and adverbs into phrases.

LESSON 46.

ANALYSIS AND PARSING.

MISCELLANEOUS.

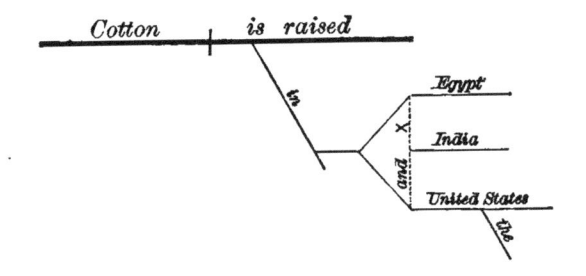

Explanation of the Diagram. — In this diagram the line representing the principal part of the phrase separates into three lines. This shows that the principal part of the phrase is compound. *Egypt, India,* and *United States* are all introduced by the same preposition *in,* and have the same relation to *is raised.*

1. Cotton is raised in Egypt, India, and the United States.
2. The navy of Hiram brought gold from Ophir.
3. The career of Cromwell was short.
4. Most mountain ranges run parallel with the coast.
5. Now swiftly glides the bonny boat.
6. An able but dishonest judge presided.
7. The queen bee lays eggs in cells of three different sizes.
8. Umbrellas were introduced into England from China.
9. The first permanent English settlement in America was made at Jamestown, in 1607.
10. The spirit of true religion is social, kind, and cheerful.
11. The summits of the Alps are covered with perpetual snow.

12. The months of July and August were named after Julius Cæsar and Augustus Cæsar.

13. All the kings of Egypt are called, in Scripture, Pharaoh.

14. The bamboo furnishes to the natives of China, shade, food, houses, weapons, and clothing.

Notice that, in 8, *were introduced* is modified by the two phrases *into England* and *from China*. The whole phrase *into England from China* is, then, a **compound phrase.**

Notice that, in 14, *natives*, the principal word of the phrase *to the natives*, is modified by another phrase, *of China*. The whole phrase *to the natives of China* is therefore a **complex phrase.**

Is there another compound or complex phrase in these fourteen sentences? Is there one in the fifteen sentences of Lesson 45?

LESSON 47.

COMPOSITION.

Supply attribute complements to the following expressions. See Caution, Lesson 40.

The marble feels ——. Mary looks ——. The weather continues ——. The apple tastes ——. That lady appears ——. The sky grows ——. The leaves of roses are ——. The undertaking was pronounced ——.

Write a subject and a predicate for each of the following nouns taken as attribute complements: —

Model. — *Soldier.* — That old man has been a *soldier.*

Plant, insect, mineral, vegetable, liquid, gas, solid, historian, poet, artist, traveler, emperor.

Using the following nouns as subjects, build sentences each having a simple predicate and two or more object complements: —

Congress, storm, education, king, tiger, hunter, Arnold, shoemakers, lawyers, merchant.

Build three sentences on each of the following subjects, two of which shall contain object complements, and the third, an attribute complement: —

Model. — *Sun.* — The *sun* gives *light.*
The *sun* warms the *earth.*
The *sun* is a luminous *body.*

Moon. oak, fire, whisky.

LESSON 48.

SUBJECT OR COMPLEMENT MODIFIED BY A PARTICIPLE.

Hints for Oral Instruction. — You have learned, in the preceding lessons, that a quality may be assumed as belonging to a thing; as, *white chalk,* or that it may be asserted of it; as, "Chalk *is white.*" An action, also, may be assumed as belonging to something; as, Peter *turning,* or it may be asserted; as, "Peter *turned.*" In the expression, "Peter, *turning, said,*" which word expresses an action as assumed, and which asserts an action? Each pupil may give an example of an action asserted and of an action assumed; as, "Corn *grows,*" corn *growing;* "Geese *gabble,*" geese *gabbling.*

Subject or Complement modified by a Participle.

This form of the verb, which merely assumes the act, being, or state, is called a **participle**.

When the words *growing* and *gabbling* are placed before the nouns, thus: *growing corn, gabbling geese*, they tell simply the kind of corn and the kind of geese, and are therefore adjectives.

When *the* or some other adjective is placed before these words, and a preposition after them, thus: *The growing of* the corn, *the gabbling of* the geese, they are simply the names of actions, and are therefore nouns.

Let each pupil give an example of a verb asserting an action, and change it to express: —

(1) An assumed action; (2) A permanent quality; (3) The name of an action.

Participles may be completed by objects and attributes.

ANALYSIS AND PARSING.

Model. — *Truth, crushed to earth, will rise again.*

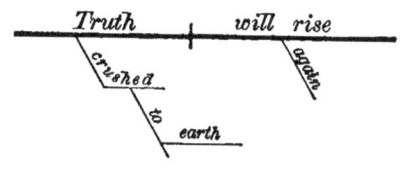

```
   Truth    |   will  rise
   \           \
    \crushed    \again
     \           
      \to
       earth
```

Explanation of the Diagram. — In this diagram, the line standing for the principal word of the participial phrase is broken; one part slants, and the other is horizontal. This shows that the participle *crushed* is used like an adjective to modify *Truth*, and yet retains the nature of a verb, expressing an action received by truth.

Oral Analysis. — This is a sentence, because ———; *Truth* is the subject, because ———; *will rise* is the predicate, because ———; the phrase, *crushed to earth,* is a modifier of the subject, because ———; *crushed* introduces the phrase and is the principal word in it; the phrase *to earth* is a modifier of *crushed; to* introduces it, and *earth* is the principal word in it; *again* is a modifier of the predicate, because ———. *Truth crushed to earth* is the modified subject, *will rise again* is the modified predicate.

Parsing. — *Crushed* is the form of the verb called participle. The action expressed by it is merely assumed.

1. The mirth of Addison is genial, imparting a mild glow of thought.
2. The general, riding to the front, led the attack.
3. The balloon, shooting swiftly into the clouds, was soon lost to sight.
4. Wealth acquired dishonestly will prove a curse.
5. The sun, rising, dispelled the mists.
6. The thief, being detected, surrendered to the officer.
7. They boarded the vessel lying in the harbor.
8. The territory claimed by the Dutch was called New Netherlands.
9. Washington, having crossed the Delaware, attacked the Hessians stationed at Trenton.
10. Burgoyne, having been surrounded at Saratoga, surrendered to General Gates.
11. Pocahontas was married to a young Englishman named John Rolfe.
12. A shrug of the shoulders, translated into words, loses much force.
13. The armies of England, mustered for the battles of Europe, do not awaken sincere admiration.

Note that the participle, like the predicate verb, may consist of two or more words.

Note, too, that the participle, like the adjective, may belong to a noun complement.

LESSON 49.

THE INFINITIVE PHRASE.

Hints for Oral Instruction. — There is another form of the verb which, like the participle, cannot be the predicate of a sentence, for it cannot assert; as, "She went out *to see* a friend;" "*To lie* is a disgrace." As this form of the verb expresses the action, being, or state in a general manner, without limiting it directly to a subject, it is called an **Infinitive,** which means without limit. The infinitive generally follows *to;* as, *to walk, to sleep*.

Let each pupil give an infinitive.

The infinitive and the preposition *to* constitute an **Infinitive phrase,** which may be employed in several ways.

T. — "I have a duty *to perform.*" The infinitive phrase modifies what? P. — The noun *duty*. T. — It then performs the office of what? P. — Of an adjective modifier.

T. — "I come *to hear*." The infinitive phrase modifies what? P. — The verb *come*. T. — What office then does it perform? P. — That of an adverb modifier.

T.—"*To lie* is base." What is base? P.—To lie.
T.—"He attempted *to speak.*" What did he attempt?
P.—To speak. T.—*To lie* is a subject, and *to speak* is an object. What part of speech is used as subject and object? P.—The noun.

T.—The **Infinitive phrase** is used as an **adjective,** an **adverb,** and a **noun.**

Infinitives may be completed by objects and attributes.

ANALYSIS AND PARSING.

Model.—*David hasted to meet Goliath.*

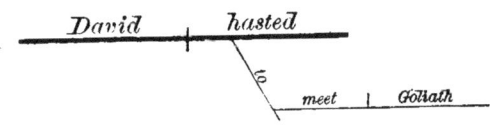

$$\underline{David \mid hasted \diagdown_{to} \underline{meet \mid Goliath}}$$

Analysis of the Infinitive Phrase.—*To* introduces the phrase; *meet,* completed by the object *Goliath,* is the principal part.

Parsing of the Phrase.—*To* is a preposition, because ———; *meet* is a verb, because ———; *Goliath* is a noun, because ———.

1. I come not here to talk.
2. I rejoice to hear it.
3. A desire to excel leads to eminence.
4. Dr. Franklin was sent to France to solicit aid for the colonies.
5. To retreat was impossible.

To here merely introduces the infinitive phrase.

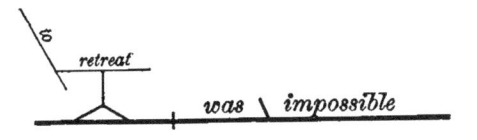

Explanation of the Diagram.—As this phrase subject cannot, in its proper form, be written on the subject line, it is placed above, and, by means of a support, the phrase diagram is made to rest on the subject line. The phrase complement may be diagramed in a similar way, and made to rest on the complement line.

6. The hands refuse to labor.
7. To live is not all of life.
8. The Puritans desired to obtain religious freedom.
9. The Romans, having conquered the world, were unable to conquer themselves.
10. Narvaez sailed from Cuba to conquer Florida.
11. Some savages of America and Africa love to wear rings in the nose.
12. Andrew Jackson, elected to succeed J. Q. Adams, was inaugurated in 1829.

LESSON 50.
POSITION AND PUNCTUATION OF THE PARTICIPIAL PHRASE.

See Lesson 37, and Caution 1 in Lesson 41. Correct these sentences, and punctuate them when corrected:—

A house was built for a clergyman having seven gables.
The old man struck the saucy boy raising a gold-headed cane.
We saw a marble bust of Sir W. Scott entering the vestibule.
Here is news from a neighbor boiled down.
I found a cent walking over the bridge.
Balboa discovered the Pacific ocean climbing to the top of a mountain.

Punctuate the following exercises:—

Cradled in the camp Napoleon was the darling of the army.
Having approved of the plan the king put it into execution.

Satan incensed with indignation stood unterrified.
My friend seeing me in need offered his services.
James being weary with his journey sat down on the wall.
The owl hid in the tree hooted through the night.

REVIEW QUESTIONS.

What binds together the sentences of a paragraph? What is the general topic? What are the sub-topics? What is a framework? How is it formed? Of what help would it be to the writer?

Give the Caution relating to the position of the phrase modifier. If phrases are of different rank, which should stand nearest to the word they modify? Illustrate. Why are phrases transposed? Illustrate their transposition for various reasons. What sentences of 1-19, Lesson 41, contain transposed prepositional phrases? What ones contain transposed adjectives? Adverbs? Nouns or pronouns used as objects? As attribute complements? What did you transpose in 19-29? What is transposed in sentences that ask questions? Give the Caution relating to the choice of prepositions. That relating to double negatives. Give examples of errors. What is a compound phrase? A complex? What is a participle? When may it become an adjective? It may be completed by what? What is an infinitive? An infinitive phrase? What offices may such a phrase perform? Illustrate. The infinitive may be completed by what? The *to* of an infinitive phrase may sometimes do what only?

COMPOSITION OF SENTENCES AND OF PARAGRAPHS.

SELECTION FROM GEORGE ELIOT.

And this is Dorlcote Mill. I must stand a minute or two here on the bridge and look at it, though the clouds are threatening and it is far on in the afternoon. Even in this leafless time of departing February, it is pleasant to look at. Perhaps the chill, damp season adds

Composition. 109

"Dorlcote Mill."

a charm to the trimly kept building, as old as the elms and chestnuts that shelter it from the northern blast.

The stream is brimful now, and half drowns the grassy fringe in front of the house. As I look at the stream, the vivid grass, the delicate, bright-green softening the outline of the great trunks and branches that gleam from under the bare purple boughs, I am in love with moistness, and envy the white ducks that are dipping their heads far into the water, unmindful of the awkward appearance they make in the drier world above.

1. And now there is the huge covered wagon, coming home with sacks of grain. 2. That honest wagoner is thinking of his dinner, which is getting sadly dry in the oven at this late hour; but he will not touch it till he has fed his horses — the strong, submissive beasts, who, I fancy, are looking mild reproach at him from between their blinkers, that he should crack his whip at them in that awful manner, as if they needed such a hint! 3. See how they stretch their shoulders up the slope toward the bridge, with all the more energy because they are so near home. 4. Look at their grand, shaggy feet, that seem to grasp the firm earth, at the patient strength of their necks bowed under the heavy collar, at the mighty muscles of their struggling haunches. 5. I should like to see them, with their moist necks freed from the harness, dipping their eager nostrils into the pond.

The Uses of Words and Groups of Words. — Notice that in sentence 1, third paragraph, the subject is placed after the predicate. Tell what *now* and *there* do. *Coming home with sacks of grain* does what? Does *coming* express action? Does it assert action? What is it? What does *home* do? Put *its* before *home* and then read the whole phrase. What other change do you find necessary? A noun is sometimes used alone to do the work of an adverb phrase, the preposition being omitted. What is the office of *minute* in the second sentence of the first paragraph? What preposition could be put in? In 2, third paragraph, the pronoun *which* stands for *dinner*. Read the sentence, using the noun instead of the pronoun. Have you now two sentences, or one? You see that *which* not only stands for *dinner*, but it joins on a sentence so as to make it describe the dinner. What does *till he has fed his horses* do? Omitting *till*, would this group of words be a sentence? What, then, joins this group, and makes it do the work of an adverb? Notice the dash after *horses*. The writer here breaks off rather suddenly and begins again, using *beasts* instead of *horses*. To *beasts* are added many descriptive words. You will learn that this noun *beasts* added to the noun *horses* is called an explanatory modifier. Notice that *I fancy* is thrown in loosely or independently and is set off by commas. All the other words beginning with *who* and ending with *hint* are joined by *who* to *beasts*. Notice that the writer makes these beasts think like persons, and so uses *who* instead of *which* or *that*. Do we ordinarily speak of looking anything? In *who are looking reproach*, what is the object complement of *are looking?* What long group of words made up of two sentences tells why the beasts are looking reproach? Read separately the main divisions of 2. What conjunction connects these? Is one of these divisions itself divided into parts by commas? Should then some mark of wider separation be put between the main divisions of 2? To build so long a sentence as 2 is venturesome. We advise young writers not to make such attempts. It is hard to write very long sentences and keep the meaning clear. In 3 the subject of *see* is *you*, which is generally omitted in a command. You are here told to see what? Break this long object complement up into two sentences. What do the horses stretch? Where do they stretch their shoulders? How do they stretch? Why do they stretch with more energy? What is the subject of *look* in 4? The phrase beginning with *at* and ending with *earth* does what? Find two other long phrases introduced by *at* and tell what they do.

That seem to grasp the firm earth goes with what? Put the noun *feet* in place of the pronoun *that* and make a separate sentence of this group. What word, then, makes an adjective modifier of this sentence and joins it to *feet?* Does *to grasp* assert action? What do you call it? It is here used as attribute complement. *Bowed under the heavy collar* describes what? Does *bowed* assert action? What do you call it?

To the Teacher. — If time permits, such exercises as the above may profitably be continued. See suggestions with preceding exercises.

Descriptive Writing. — This extract from the novelist who called herself "George Eliot" we have slightly changed for our purpose. It is purely **descriptive**. It is a painting in words — a vivid picture of a very pretty scene. How grateful we are to those who can, as it were, turn a page of a book into canvas, and paint on it a rich verbal picture that delights us every time we read it or recall it! How many such pictures there are in our libraries! And how little they cost us when compared with those that we buy and hang upon our walls!

Some Features of a Good Description. — Does this author mention many features of the mill, of the stream, and of the horses pulling their load over the bridge? Do those that she does mention suggest to you everything else? Name some of the things suggested to you but not mentioned in this description. Does not some of the charm of a description lie in the reader's having something left him to supply? If the author had given you every little detail of the mill, the stream, and the laboring horses, would not the description have been dull and tiresome? What things that the author imagined but did not really see are mentioned in the third paragraph? Do these touches of fancy or imagination help the picture? Do they show that the author was in love with her work? and do they therefore stimulate your fancy or imagination?

The Framework. — In making a framework for this description would you take for the general topic "The Scene from the Bridge" or "Things Seen from a Bridge"? or would you prefer some other wording of it? Now write out a framework, placing the sub-topics under the general topic as you have been taught.

Original Composition.

Describe some scene that you greatly enjoy, or draw your picture from imagination. Make a framework and try to profit by all that we have said.

LESSON 51.

REVIEW.

Correct these miscellaneous errors. See Cautions in Lessons 30, 40, and 41: —

>There never was such another man.
>He was an old venerable patriarch.
>John has a cadaverous, hungry, and lean look.
>He was a well-proportioned, fine fellow.
>Pass me them potatoes.
>Put your trust not in money.
>We have often occasion for thanksgiving.
>Now this is to be done how?
>Nothing can justify ever profanity.
>To continually study is impossible.

An adverb is seldom placed between the preposition *to* and the infinitive.

>Mary likes to tastefully dress.
>Learn to carefully choose your words.
>She looks queerly.

Give me a soon and direct answer.
The post stood firmly.
The eagle flies highly.
The orange tastes sweetly.
I feel tolerable well.
The branch breaks easy.
Thistles grow rapid.
The eagle flies swift.
This is a miserable poor pen.
A wealthy gentleman will adopt a little boy with a small family.
A gentleman called from Africa to pay his compliments.
Water consists in oxygen and hydrogen.
He went out attended with a servant.
I have a dislike to such tricksters.
We have no prejudice to foreigners.
She don't know nothing about it.
Father wouldn't give me none.
He hasn't been sick neither.
I won't have no more nohow.

To the Teacher.—See that a good reason is given for every correction.

LESSON 52.

COMPOSITION.

Build sentences in which the following participles shall be used as modifiers:—

Being fatigued; laughing; being amused; having been elected; running; having been running.

Expand each of the following sentences into three sentences, using the participial form of the verb as a participle in the first, the same form as an adjective in the second; and as a noun in the third : —

Model. — The stream *flows;* The stream, *flowing* gently, crept through the meadow; The *flowing* stream slipped away to the sea; The *flowing* of the stream caused a low murmur.

The stream flows. The sun rises. Insects hum. The birds sing. The wind whistles. The bells are ringing. The tide ebbs.

Form infinitive phrases from the following verbs, and use these phrases as adjectives, adverbs, and nouns, in sentences of your own : —

Smoke, dance, burn, eat, lie, try.

LESSON 53.

NOUNS AND PRONOUNS AS MODIFIERS.

Hints for Oral Instruction. — In the sentence, "The *robin's eggs* are blue," the noun *robin's* does what? P. — It tells what or whose eggs are blue. T. — What word names the things owned or possessed? P. — *Eggs*. T. — What word names the owner or possessor? P. — *Robin's*.

T. — The noun *robin's* is here used as a modifier. You see that this word, which I have written on the board, is the word *robin* with a little mark (') called an apostrophe, and the letter **s** added. These are added to denote possession.

In the sentence, "*Webster, the statesman*, was born in New Hampshire," the noun *statesman* modifies the subject *Webster* by explaining what or which Webster is meant. Both words name the same person.

Let the pupils give examples of each of these two kinds of **Noun Modifiers** — the **Possessive** and the **Explanatory**.

ANALYSIS AND PARSING.

Model. — *Julia's sister Mary has lost her diamond ring.*

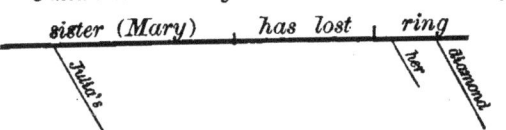

```
sister (Mary)  |  has lost  |  ring
   \Julia's                    \her \diamond
```

Explanation of the Diagram. — *Mary* is written on the subject line, because *Mary* and *sister* both name the same person, but the word *Mary* is inclosed within marks of parenthesis to show that *sister* is the proper grammatical subject.

In **oral analysis**, call *Julia's* and *Mary* modifiers of the subject, *sister*, because *Julia's* tells whose sister, and *Mary* explains *sister* by adding another name of the same person. *Her* is a modifier of the object, because it tells whose ring is meant.

Julia's sister Mary is the modified subject, the predicate is unmodified, and *her diamond ring* is the modified object complement.

1. The planet Jupiter has four moons.
2. The Emperor Nero was a cruel tyrant.
3. Peter's wife's mother lay sick of a fever.

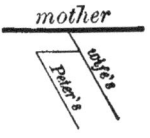

```
        mother
     \Peter's \wife's
```

4. An ostrich outruns an Arab's horse.

5. His pretty little nephew Arthur had the best claim to the throne.

6. Milton, the great English poet, became blind.

7. Cæsar gave his daughter Julia in marriage to Pompey.

8. London, the capital of England, is the largest and richest city in the world.

9. Joseph, Jacob's favorite son, was sold by his brethren to the Ishmaelites.

10. Alexander the Great[1] was educated under the celebrated philosopher, Aristotle.

11. Friends tie their purses with a spider's thread.

12. Cæsar married Cornelia, the daughter of Cinna.

13. His fate, alas! was deplorable.

14. Love rules his kingdom without a sword.

LESSON 54.

COMPOSITION.

Nouns and pronouns denoting possession may generally be changed to equivalent phrases; as, *Arnold's treason = the treason of Arnold.* Here the preposition *of* indicates possession, the relation expressed by the apostrophe (') and **s**. Change the following possessive nouns to equivalent phrases, and the phrases indicating possession to possessive nouns, and then expand the expressions into complete sentences:—

---

[1] *Alexander the Great* may be taken as one name, or *Great* may be called an explanatory modifier of *Alexander*.

Model. — The *earth's* surface; the surface *of the earth* is made up of land and water.

The earth's surface; Solomon's temple; England's King; Washington's Farewell Address; Dr. Kane's Explorations; Peter's wife's mother; George's friend's father; Shakespeare's plays; Noah's dove; the diameter of the earth; the daughter of Jephthah; the invasion of Burgoyne; the voyage of Cabot; the Armada of Philip; the attraction of the earth; the light of the moon.

Find for the things mentioned below, other names which shall describe or explain them. Add such names to these nouns, and then expand the expressions into complete sentences: —

Model. — Ink. — *Ink, a dark fluid,* is used in writing.

Observe the following rule: —

Comma — Rule. — An **Explanatory Modifier**, when it does not restrict the modified term or combine closely with it, is set off by the comma.

New York, rain, paper, the monkey, the robin, tea, Abraham Lincoln, Alexander Hamilton, world, peninsula, Cuba, Shakespeare.

The chief difficulty in the punctuation of the different kinds of modifiers is in determining whether or not they are restrictive. The following examples illustrate the difficulty: —

(a) The words *golden* and *oriole* are pleasant to the ear.
(b) Words, the signs of ideas, are spoken and written.
(c) Use words that are current.

(*d*) Words, which are the signs of ideas, are spoken and written.

(*e*) The country anciently called Gaul is now called France.

(*f*) France, anciently called Gaul, derived its name from the Franks.

(*g*) Glass bends easily when it is hot.

(*h*) I met him in Paris, when I was last abroad.

In (*a*) the application of *words* is limited, or restricted, to the two words mentioned; in (*c*) *words* is **restricted to a certain kind.** In (*b*) and (*d*) the modifiers **do not restrict**. They apply to all words and simply **add information.** In (*e*) the participial phrase restricts the application of *country* to one particular country; but in (*f*) the phrase describes without limiting. The omission of the comma in (*g*) shows that "*Glass bends easily*" is not offered as a general statement, but that the action is restricted to a certain time or condition. *When it is hot* is essential to the intended meaning. The punctuation of (*h*) shows that the speaker does not wish to make the time of meeting a prominent or essential part of what he has to say. The adverb clause simply gives additional information. If (*h*) were an answer to the question, When did you meet him? the comma would be omitted. The sense may be varied by the use or the omission of the comma.

Let the pupils see how incomplete the statements are when the restrictive modifiers are omitted, and that the other modifiers are not so necessary to the sense, but are supplementary. In such expressions as *I myself, we boys,* the explanatory words are not restrictive, but they combine closely with the modified term.

Write three sentences, each of which shall contain a noun or pronoun denoting possession, and a noun or pronoun used to explain.

Study these possessive forms with reference to the possessive signs: —

The sailor's story; the farmer's son; the pony's mane; the monkey's tail; a day's work; James's book; a cent's worth; a man's wages; the child's toys; the woman's hat; the sailors' stories; the farmers' sons; the ponies' manes; the monkeys' tails; three days' work; five cents' worth; two men's wages; those children's toys; women's hats.

Pick out the nouns above that are in the singular and tell which of the two possessive signs — ('s) or (') — they add. Which do nouns in the plural add? Note, above, three exceptions in the plural. *Man, woman,* and *child* do not add the regular s-ending to form their plurals. The plurals are *men, women,* and *children,* and the possessive form of these has the full ('s) — as is seen above.

Study these possessive forms: —

Dombey & Son's business; J. J. Little & Co.'s printing-house; William the Conqueror's reign; Reed and Kellogg's series of grammars are Maynard, Merrill, & Company's publications.

When a group of words is treated as a compound name, which word of the group takes the possessive sign?

LESSON 55.
ANALYSIS AND PARSING.
Miscellaneous Examples in Review.

1. The toad spends the winter in a dormant state.
2. Pride in dress or in beauty betrays a weak mind.
3. The city of London is situated on the river Thames.
4. Napoleon Bonaparte was born in 1769, on an island in the Mediterranean.
5. Men's opinions vary with their interests.
6. Ammonia is found in the sap of trees, and in the juices of all vegetables.
7. Earth sends up her perpetual hymn of praise to the Creator.
8. Having once been deceived by him, I never trusted him again.
9. Æsop, the author of Æsop's Fables, was a slave.
10. Hope comes with smiles to cheer the hour of pain.
11. Clouds are collections of vapors in the air.
12. To relieve the wretched was his pride.
13. Greece, the most noted country of antiquity, scarcely exceeded in size the half of the state of New York.

What phrases above are (1) adjectival, (2) adverbial, (3) compound, and (4) complex? What compound phrase has a complex as a part of it?

LESSON 56.
ANALYSIS AND PARSING.
Miscellaneous Examples in Review — continued.

1. We are never too old to learn.
2. Civility is the result of good nature and good sense.

3. The right of the people to instruct their representatives is generally admitted.

4. The immense quantity of matter in the Universe presents a most striking display of Almighty power.

5. Virtue, diligence, and industry, joined with good temper and prudence, must ever be the surest means of prosperity.

6. The people called Quakers were a source of much trouble to the Puritans.

7. The Mayflower brought to America [1] one hundred and one men, women, and children.

8. Edward Wingfield, an avaricious and unprincipled man, was the first president of the Jamestown colony.

9. John Cabot and his son Sebastian, sailing under a commission from Henry VII. of England, discovered the continent of America.

10. True worth is modest and retiring.

11. Jonah, the prophet, preached to the inhabitants of Nineveh.

In the exercise you take for pleasure, in the errands on which you are sent, and in your going to and from school, I will suppose that, like the girl in the picture, you walk; or, like the boy in the picture, you ride on your wheel.

We are all reasonable beings. This means that, whether or not we think of it at the time, we always have a reason for everything we do. If we walk, we do it for reasons that seem good to us; if we ride, we do it for other reasons that seem good to us.

Now, without suggestions from any one, think, if possible, of at least four reasons, satisfactory to you, why

---

[1] *One hundred and one* may be taken as one adjective.

A GIRL ON FOOT AND A BOY SPINNING BY ON A WHEEL.

you go about on foot, if you do; why you go about on a wheel, if you do — reasons which you can urge in defence and justification of your method of locomotion. These reasons will form an **Argument**.

Then under the heading, or topic,

WHY I GO ABOUT ON FOOT,
OR
WHY I GO ABOUT ON A WHEEL,

array, one after another, in the most natural order you can think of, these good reasons, each beginning, "I walk because," etc.; or "I ride on a wheel because," etc. Then expand each reason into a paragraph.

These reasons, or **sub-topics,** in proper order, numbered, and standing under the **general topic,** form an **outline** or **framework.** The development of each sub-topic forms, as we have seen, a **paragraph,** which is made up of sentences in proper order. The relative **length** of the paragraphs depends upon the relative importance of the sub-topics; and the paragraphs grouped together constitute a **composition,** or theme.

LESSON 57.

COMPLEX SENTENCES.

THE ADJECTIVE CLAUSE.

Hints for Oral Instruction.—A word-modifier may sometimes be expanded into a phrase or into an expression that asserts.

T.—"A *wise* man will be honored." Expand *wise* into a phrase, and give me the sentence. **P.**—"A man *of wisdom* will be honored." **T.**—Expand *wise* into an expression that asserts, join this to *man,* as a modifier, and then give me the entire sentence. **P.**—"A man *who is wise* will be honored."

T.—You see that the same quality may be expressed in three ways—A *wise* man, A man *of wisdom,* A man *who is wise.*

Complex Sentences.

Let the pupils give similar examples.

T. — In the sentence, "A man *who is wise* will be honored," the word *who* stands for what? **P.** — For the noun *man*. **T.** — Then what part of speech is it? **P.** — A pronoun.

T. — Put the noun *man* in the place of the pronoun *who*, and then give me the sentence. **P.** — "*A man, man is wise*, will be honored."

T. — I will repeat your sentence, changing the order of the words — "*A man will be honored.*" "*Man is wise.*" Is the last sentence now joined to the first as a modifier, or are they two separate sentences? **P.** — They are two separate sentences.

T. — Then you see that the pronoun *who* not only stands for the noun *man*, but it connects the modifying expression, *who is wise*, to *man*, the subject of the sentence, "*A man will be honored*," and thus there is formed what we call a **Complex Sentence**. These two parts we call **Clauses**. "*A man will be honored*" is the **Independent Clause**; *who is wise* is the **Dependent Clause**.

Clauses that modify nouns or pronouns are called **Adjective Clauses.**

DEFINITION. — A **Clause** is a part of a sentence containing a subject and its predicate.

DEFINITION. — A **Dependent Clause** is one used as an adjective, an adverb, or a noun.

DEFINITION. — An **Independent Clause** is one not dependent on another clause.

DEFINITION. — A **Simple Sentence** is one that contains but one subject and one predicate, either or both of which may be compound.

DEFINITION. — A **Complex Sentence** is one composed of an independent clause and one or more dependent clauses.

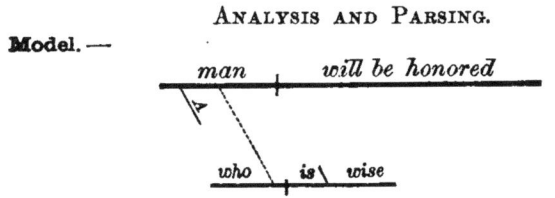

ANALYSIS AND PARSING.

Model. —

```
    man    |  will be honored
   /
  /
 who  \  is \  wise
```

Explanation of the Diagram. — You will notice that the lines standing for the subject and predicate of the independent clause are heavier than those of the dependent clause. This pictures to you the relative importance of the two clauses. You will see that the pronoun *who* is written on the subject line of the dependent clause. But this word performs the office of a conjunction also, and this office is expressed in the diagram by a dotted line. As all modifiers are joined by slanting lines to the words they modify, you learn from this diagram that *who is wise* is a modifier of *man*.

Oral Analysis. — This is a complex sentence, because it consists of an independent clause and a dependent clause. "*A man will be honored*" is the independent clause; *who is wise* is the dependent clause. *Man* is the subject of the independent clause; *will be honored* is the predicate. The word *A* and the clause, *who is wise*, are modifiers of the subject. *A* points out *man*, and *who is wise* tells the kind of man. *A man who is wise* is the modified subject; the predicate is unmodified. *Who* is the subject of the dependent clause, *is* is the predicate, and *wise* is the attribute complement. *Who* connects the two clauses.

1. He that runs may read.
2. Man is the only animal that laughs and weeps.
3. Henry Hudson discovered the river which bears his name.
4. He necessarily remains weak who never tries exertion.
5. The meridians are those lines that extend from pole to pole.
6. He who will not be ruled by the rudder must be ruled by the rock.
7. Animals that have a backbone are called vertebrates.
8. Uneasy lies the head that wears a crown.
9. The thick mists which prevail in the neighborhood of Newfoundland are caused by the warm waters of the Gulf Stream.
10. The power which brings a pin to the ground holds the earth in its orbit.
11. Death is the black camel which kneels at every man's gate.
12. Our best friends are they who tell us of our faults, and help us to mend them.

The pupil will notice that, in some of these sentences, the dependent clause modifies the subject, and that, in others, it modifies the noun complement.

COMMA — RULE. — The **adjective** or the **adverb clause**, when it does not closely follow and restrict the word modified, is generally set off by the comma.

LESSON 58.

COMPOSITION.

ADJECTIVE CLAUSES.

Expand each of the following adjectives into

(1) A phrase, (2) A clause.

and then use these three modifiers in three separate sentences of your own construction: —

Model. — *Energetic; of energy;* { *who has energy,* or *who is energetic.* }

An *energetic* man will succeed; a man *of energy* will succeed; a man *who has energy* (or *who is energetic*) will succeed.

Honest, long-eared, beautiful, wealthy.

Expand each of the following possessive nouns into

(1) A phrase, (2) A clause,

and then use these three modifiers in three separate sentences: —

Model. — *Saturn's* rings; the rings *of Saturn;* the rings *which surround Saturn.*

Saturn's rings can be seen with a telescope; the rings *of Saturn* can be seen with a telescope; the rings *which surround Saturn* can be seen with a telescope.

Absalom's hair; the hen's eggs; the elephant's tusks.

Change the following simple sentences into complex sentences by expanding the participial phrases into clauses.

The vessels carrying the blood from the heart are called arteries.
The book prized above all other books is the Bible.
Rivers rising west of the Rocky Mts. flow into the Pacific ocean.
The guns fired at Concord were heard around the world.

LESSON 59.

COMPLEX SENTENCES.

THE ADVERB CLAUSE.

Hints for Oral Instruction. — You learned in Lesson 33 that an adverb can be expanded into an equivalent phrase; as, "The book was *carefully* read" = "The book was read *with care.*"

You are now to learn that a phrase used as an adverb may be expanded into an **Adverb clause**. In the sentence, "We started *at sunrise*," what phrase is used like an adverb? P.—*At sunrise.* T.—Expand this phrase into an equivalent clause, and give me the entire sentence. P.—"We started *when the sun rose.*"

T.—You see that the phrase, *at sunrise*, and the clause, *when the sun rose*, both modify *started*, telling the time of starting, and are therefore equivalent to adverbs. We will then call such clauses **Adverb clauses**.

ANALYSIS AND PARSING.

Model.—

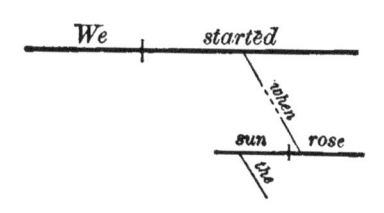

We | started
 \ when
  sun | rose
   \ the

Explanation of the Diagram. — The line which connects the two predicate lines pictures three things. It is made up of three parts. The upper part shows that *when* modifies *started;* the lower part, that it modifies *rose;* and the dotted part shows that it connects.

Oral Analysis — This is a complex sentence, because ———; *We started* is the independent clause, and *when the sun rose* is the dependent clause. *We* is the subject of the independent clause, and *started* is the predicate. The clause, *when the sun rose*, is a modifier of the predicate, because it tells when we started. *Started when the sun rose* is the modified predicate.

Sun is the subject of the dependent clause, and *rose* is the predicate, and *the* is a modifier of *sun; the sun* is the modified subject. *When* modifies *rose* and *started*, and connects the clause-modifier to the predicate *started*.

Parsing of *when*. — *When* is an adverb modifying the two verbs *started* and *rose*, and thus connects the two clauses. It modifies these verbs by showing that the two actions took place at the same time.

1. The dew glitters when the sun shines.
2. Printing was unknown when Homer wrote the Iliad.
3. Where the bee sucks honey, the spider sucks poison.
4. Ah! few shall part where many meet.
5. Where the devil cannot come, he will send.
6. While the bridegroom tarried, they all slumbered and slept.
7. Fools rush in where angels fear to tread.
8. When the tale of bricks is doubled, Moses comes.
9. When I look upon the tombs of the great, every emotion of envy dies within me.
10. The upright man speaks as he thinks.
11. He died as the fool dieth.
12. The scepter shall not depart from Judah until Shiloh come.

When, while, and *until* indicate time; the clauses they introduce are **adverb clauses of time**. Select them. *Where* indicates place; the clauses it introduces are **adverb clauses of place**. How many are there in the sentences above? *As* here indicates manner. Pick out the **adverb clauses of manner** which it introduces. In

> The ground is wet *because* it rains; *if* the night is cloudy, no dew will fall; *though* it rained during the night, the ground is now dry; Nature puts us to sleep at night *that* she may repair the waste of the body by day,

the clauses introduced by (1) *because*, (2) *if*, (3) *though*, and (4) *that* are **adverb clauses of** (1) **cause**, (2) **condition**, (3) **concession**, and (4) **purpose**. The words introducing them are not conjunctive adverbs but pure conjunctions, and stand where *when* stands, in the diagram above, but on a line dotted throughout.

See if, in the offices which these common adverb clauses perform, you can find the justification of their names.

LESSON 60.

COMPOSITION.

Adverb Clauses.

Expand each of the following phrases into an adverb clause, and fit this clause into a sentence of your own:—

Model. — *At sunset; when the sun set.* We returned *when the sun set.*

At the hour; on the playground; by moonlight; in youth; among icebergs; after school; at the forks of the road; during the day; before church; with my friend.

To each of the following independent clauses, join an adverb clause, and so make complex sentences:—

——— Peter began to sink. The man dies ———. Grass grows ———. Iron ——— can easily be shaped. The rattlesnake shakes his rattle ———. ——— a nation mourns. Pittsburg stands ———. He dared to lead ———.

An adverb clause may stand before the independent clause, between its parts, or after it; as, "*When it is hot*, glass bends easily"; "Glass, *when it is hot*, bends easily"; "Glass bends easily *when it is hot*." Notice the punctuation of these examples.

Adverb clauses may be contracted in various ways. Clauses introduced by the comparatives *as* and *than* are usually found in an abbreviated form; as, "You are as old *as* he (*is old*)"; "You are older *than* I (*am old*)." Attention may be called to the danger of mistaking here the nominative for the objective. We suggest making selections for the study of adverb clauses.

REVIEW QUESTIONS.

In what two ways may nouns be used as modifiers? Illustrate. Nouns and pronouns denoting possession may sometimes be changed into what? Illustrate. Give the rule for the punctuation of explanatory modifiers. Into what may an adjective be expanded? Into what may a participial phrase be expanded? Give illustrations.

Give an example of a complex sentence. Of a clause. Of an independent clause. Of a dependent clause. Into what may a phrase used as an adverb be expanded? Illustrate the seven classes of adverb clauses spoken of in Lesson 59.

Composition of Sentences and of Paragraphs.
SELECTION FROM THE BROTHERS GRIMM.

Once upon a time there was a very old man, whose eyes were dim, whose ears were dull, and whose knees trembled. When he sat at table, he could scarcely hold his spoon; and often he spilled his food over the tablecloth and sometimes down his clothes.

His son and daughter-in-law were much vexed about this, and at last they made the old man sit behind the oven in a corner, and gave him his food in an earthen dish, and not enough of it either; so that the poor man grew sad, and his eyes were wet with tears. Once his hand trembled so much that he could not hold the dish, and it fell upon the ground and broke all in pieces, so that the young wife scolded him; but he made no reply and only sighed. Then they bought him a wooden dish, and out of that he had to feed.

One day, as he was sitting in his usual place, he saw his little grandson, four years old, fitting together some pieces of wood. "What are you making?" asked the old man.

"I am making a wooden trough," replied the child, "for father and mother to feed out of when I grow big."

At these words the father looked at his wife for a moment, and presently they began to cry. Henceforth they let the old grandfather sit at table with them, and they did not even say anything if he spilled a little food upon the cloth.

The Uses of Words and Groups of Words. — What is the order of subject and predicate in the first sentence of this selection? The word *there* does not tell where; it is put before *was* to let the subject follow. *There* is frequently so used and is then called an independent adverb. Find in the first sentence three adjective clauses. What connects each to *man?* What other office has this connective? How are these adjective clauses connected with one another? What is the office of the dependent clause in the next sentence? If this clause were placed after its principal clause, would the comma be needed? Are the clauses separated by the semicolon as closely connected as those divided by the comma?

After *made* and some other words the *to* before the infinitive is omitted. Find such an instance in the first sentence of the second paragraph. In this same sentence change *gave him his food*, making *him* come last. You have learned that a noun or a pronoun may be used without a preposition to do the work of an adverb phrase.

Composition. 135

What does *one day* do in the third paragraph? Is a preposition needed before *day*? In the same sentence *years* is used adverbially to modify the adjective *old*. It would be hard to find a preposition to put before *years*. We might say "old to the extent of four years," but *four years* answers for the whole phrase. In this same paragraph what words are quoted exactly as the old man uttered them? Notice that the next quotation is broken by the words *replied the child*, and so each part of the quotation is separately inclosed within quotation marks. (See next lesson.)

To the Teacher. — We have here touched a few features of the sentences above. The exercises given with the preceding selections will suggest a fuller examination of the phrases and clauses.

Suggestions from this Narrative. — We see that this beautiful story has a purpose. Its purpose is to teach us kindness to our parents. It is well planned. Every sentence and every paragraph is adapted to the end in view. No useless item or circumstance is admitted. The story stops when the end is reached. Anything added to the fifth paragraph would spoil the story. We certainly can learn much from such a model.

Paragraphs. — Does every sentence in the first paragraph aid in picturing the helplessness of the old grandfather? Is the picture complete? Does the second paragraph strongly impress us with the unkindness of the son and daughter-in-law, who ought to have been moved to pity by the old man's condition? Does it contain an unnecessary sentence? In telling how the grandchild unconsciously taught a lesson, a dialogue is introduced, and so what really belongs to one sub-topic is put in the form of two paragraphs. It is customary to make a separate paragraph of each single speech in a dialogue. Read the last paragraph carefully and see whether one could wish to know anything more about the effect of the lesson taught by the child.

Make a **framework** for this story.

ORIGINAL COMPOSITION.

Make up a short story from your own experience, or from your imagination, and try to profit by the suggestions above. Prepare a framework at the beginning.

LESSON 61.

THE NOUN CLAUSE.

Hints for Oral Instruction.—"*That stars are suns* is taught by astronomers." What is taught by astronomers? P.—That stars are suns. T.—What, then, is the subject of *is taught?* P.—The clause, *That stars are suns.* T.—This clause, then, performs the office of what part of speech? P.—Of a noun.

T.—"Astronomers teach *that stars are suns.*" What do astronomers teach? P.—That stars are suns. T.—What is the object complement of *teach?* P.—The clause, *that stars are suns.* T.—What office, then, does this clause perform? P.—That of a noun.

T.—"The teaching of astronomers is, *that stars are suns.*" What does *is* assert of teaching? P.—That stars are suns. T.—What, then, is the attribute complement? P.—*That stars are suns.* T.—Does this complement express the quality of the subject, or does it name the thing that the subject names? P.—It names the thing that the subject names. T.—It is equivalent then to what part of speech? P.—To a noun.

The Noun Clause.

T. — You see then that a clause, like a noun, may be used as the subject or the complement of a sentence.

ANALYSIS AND PARSING.

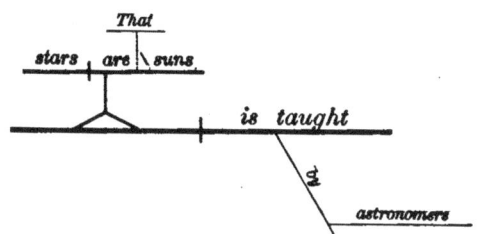

You will understand this diagram from the explanation of the second diagram in Lesson 49.

Oral Analysis. — This is a complex sentence, in which the whole sentence takes the place of the independent clause. *That stars are suns* is the dependent clause. *That stars are suns* is the subject of the whole sentence. *That* simply introduces the dependent clause.

In **parsing**, call *that* a conjunction.

1. That the Scotch are an intelligent people is generally acknowledged.
2. That the moon is made of green cheese is believed by some boys and girls.
3. That Julius Cæsar invaded Britain is a historic fact.
4. That children should obey their parents is a divine precept.
5. I know that my Redeemer liveth.
6. Plato taught that the soul is immortal.
7. Peter denied that he knew his Lord.
8. Mahomet found that the mountain would not move.
9. The principle maintained by the colonies was, that taxation without representation is unjust.

10. Our intention is, that this work shall be well done.
11. Our hearts' desire and prayer is, that you may be saved.
12. The belief of the Sadducees was, that there is no resurrection of the dead.

Look at the noun clauses in these sentences: —

1. Goldsmith says, "Learn the luxury of doing good."
2. Goldsmith says that we should learn the luxury of doing good.
3. "The owlet Atheism, hooting at the glorious sun in heaven, cries out, 'Where is it?'"
4. Coleridge compares atheism to an owlet hooting at the sun, and asking where it is.
5. "To read without reflecting," says Burke, "is like eating without digesting."
6. May we not find "sermons in stones and good in everything"?
7. There is much meaning in the following quotation: "Books are embalmed minds."
8. We must ask, What are we living for?
9. We must ask what we are living for.

Notice that the writer of (1) has copied into his sentence (quoted) the exact language of Goldsmith. The two marks, like inverted commas, and the two marks, like apostrophes, which inclose this copied passage (quotation), are called **Quotation Marks**.

Name all the differences between (1) and (2). Is the same thought expressed in both? Which quotation would you call **direct**? Which, **indirect**?

Notice that the whole of (3) is a quotation, and that this quotation contains another quotation inclosed within single marks. Notice the order of the marks at the end of (3).

Point out the differences between (3) and (4). In which is a question quoted just as it would be asked? In which is a question merely referred to? Which question would you call direct? Which, indirect? Name every difference in the form of these.

In which of the above sentences is a quotation interrupted by a parenthetical clause? How are the parts marked?

Point out a quotation that cannot make complete sense by itself. How does it differ from the others as to punctuation and the first letter?

In (7) a Colon precedes the quotation to show that it is introduced in a formal manner by the word *following*.

In (8) a question is introduced without quotation marks. Questions that, like this, are introduced without being referred to any particular person or persons, are often written without quotation marks. State the differences between (8) and (9).

In quoting a question, the interrogation point must stand within the quotation marks; but, when a question contains a quotation, this order is reversed. Point out illustrations above.

Selections written in the colloquial style and containing frequent quotations and questions may be taken from reading books, for examination, discussion, and copying.

Explanation of the Diagram. — The line which connects the two predicate lines pictures three things. It is made up of three parts. The upper part shows that *when* modifies *started;* the lower part, that it modifies *rose;* and the dotted part shows that it connects.

Oral Analysis — This is a complex sentence, because——; *We started* is the independent clause, and *when the sun rose* is the dependent clause. *We* is the subject of the independent clause, and *started* is the predicate. The clause, *when the sun rose*, is a modifier of the predicate, because it tells when we started. *Started when the sun rose* is the modified predicate.

Sun is the subject of the dependent clause, and *rose* is the predicate, and *the* is a modifier of *sun; the sun* is the modified subject. *When* modifies *rose* and *started*, and connects the clause-modifier to the predicate *started*.

Parsing of *when.* — *When* is an adverb modifying the two verbs *started* and *rose*, and thus connects the two clauses. It modifies these verbs by showing that the two actions took place at the same time.

1. The dew glitters when the sun shines.
2. Printing was unknown when Homer wrote the Iliad.
3. Where the bee sucks honey, the spider sucks poison.
4. Ah! few shall part where many meet.
5. Where the devil cannot come, he will send.
6. While the bridegroom tarried, they all slumbered and slept.
7. Fools rush in where angels fear to tread.
8. When the tale of bricks is doubled, Moses comes.
9. When I look upon the tombs of the great, every emotion of envy dies within me.
10. The upright man speaks as he thinks.
11. He died as the fool dieth.
12. The scepter shall not depart from Judah until Shiloh come.

When, while, and *until* indicate time; the clauses they introduce are **adverb clauses of time.** Select them. *Where* indicates place; the clauses it introduces are **adverb clauses of place.** How many are there in the sentences above? *As* here indicates manner. Pick out the adverb clauses of manner which it introduces. In

The ground is wet *because* it rains; *if* the night is cloudy, no dew will fall; *though* it rained during the night, the ground is now dry; Nature puts us to sleep at night *that* she may repair the waste of the body by day,

the clauses introduced by (1) *because,* (2) *if,* (3) *though,* and (4) *that* are **adverb clauses of** (1) **cause,** (2) **condition,** (3) **concession,** and (4) **purpose.** The words introducing them are not conjunctive adverbs but pure conjunctions, and stand where *when* stands, in the diagram above, but on a line dotted throughout.

See if, in the offices which these common adverb clauses perform, you can find the justification of their names.

LESSON 60.

COMPOSITION.

ADVERB CLAUSES.

Expand each of the following phrases into an adverb clause, and fit this clause into a sentence of your own: —

Model. — *At sunset; when the sun set.* We returned *when the sun set.*

At the hour; on the playground; by moonlight; in youth; among icebergs; after school; at the forks of the road; during the day; before church; with my friend.

To each of the following independent clauses, join an adverb clause, and so make complex sentences: —

——— Peter began to sink. The man dies ———. Grass grows ———. Iron ——— can easily be shaped. The rattlesnake shakes his rattle ———. ——— a nation mourns. Pittsburg stands ———. He dared to lead ———.

An adverb clause may stand before the independent clause, between its parts, or after it; as, "*When it is hot*, glass bends easily"; "Glass, *when it is hot*, bends easily"; "Glass bends easily *when it is hot*." Notice the punctuation of these examples.

Adverb clauses may be contracted in various ways. Clauses introduced by the comparatives *as* and *than* are usually found in an abbreviated form; as, "You are as old *as* he (*is old*)"; "You are older *than* I (*am old*)." Attention may be called to the danger of mistaking here the nominative for the objective. We suggest making selections for the study of adverb clauses.

REVIEW QUESTIONS.

In what two ways may nouns be used as modifiers? Illustrate. Nouns and pronouns denoting possession may sometimes be changed into what? Illustrate. Give the rule for the punctuation of explanatory modifiers. Into what may an adjective be expanded? Into what may a participial phrase be expanded? Give illustrations.

Give an example of a complex sentence. Of a clause. Of an independent clause. Of a dependent clause. Into what may a phrase used as an adverb be expanded? Illustrate the seven classes of adverb clauses spoken of in Lesson 59.

COMPOSITION OF SENTENCES AND OF PARAGRAPHS.

SELECTION FROM THE BROTHERS GRIMM.

Once upon a time there was a very old man, whose eyes were dim, whose ears were dull, and whose knees trembled. When he sat at table, he could scarcely hold his spoon; and often he spilled his food over the tablecloth and sometimes down his clothes.

His son and daughter-in-law were much vexed about this, and at last they made the old man sit behind the oven in a corner, and gave

10. [1]Cassius, be not deceived.

11. How rich, how poor, how abject, how august, how wonderful is man!

12. Which is the largest city in the world?

LESSON 65.

ANALYSIS AND PARSING.

Miscellaneous Exercises in Review — Continued.

1. Politeness is the oil which lubricates the wheels of society.

2. O liberty! liberty! how many crimes are committed in thy name!

3. The mind is a goodly field, and to sow it with trifles is the worst husbandry in the world.

4. Every day in thy life is a leaf in thy history.

5. Make hay while the sun shines.

6. Columbus did not know that he had discovered a new continent.

7. The subject of inquiry was, Who invented printing?

8. The cat's tongue is covered with thousands of little sharp cones, pointing towards the throat.

9. The fly sat upon the axle of a chariot wheel and said, "What a dust do I raise!"

10. Sir Humphrey Gilbert, attempting to recross the Atlantic in his little vessel, the Squirrel, went down in mid-ocean.

11. Charity begins at home, but it should not stay there.

12. The morn, in russet mantle clad, walks o'er the dew of yon high eastern hill.

---

[1] *Cassius* is independent, and may be diagramed like an interjection. The subject of *be deceived*, is *thou* or *you*, understood.

"At Recess."

This is a picture of pupils playing games at recess. Some of the games boys alone play; some, girls play; and some, boys and girls together play.

The boys of the class may select at least three of these games, and in as many paragraphs may tell how they are played — what they are; the girls may take the three or more which they like best, and do the same with them.

Confine yourselves to the essential features of each game. See how much good thought upon these points you can put into the paragraphs. Choose apt and simple words, arrange them with care, and diversify your sentences in kind and in length, making what you have to say clear and strong by your way of saying it.

The composition, telling what some things are, will be Expository.

LESSON 66.

MISCELLANEOUS ERRORS IN REVIEW.

I haven't near so much. I only want one. Draw the string tightly. He writes good. I will prosecute him who sticks bills upon this church or any other nuisance. Noah for his godliness and his family were saved from the flood. We were at Europe this summer. You may rely in that. She lives to home. I can't do no work. He will never be no better. They seemed to be nearly dressed alike. I won't never do so no more. A ivory ball. An hundred head of cattle. george washington. gen dix of n y. o sarah i Saw A pretty Bonnet. are You going home? A young man wrote these verses who has long lain in his grave for his own amusement. This house will be kept by the widow of Mr. B. who died recently on an improved plan. (In correcting the position of the adjective clauses in the two examples above, observe the caution for the phrase modifiers, Lesson 41.) He was an independent small farmer. The mind knows feels and thinks. The urchin was ragged barefooted dirty homeless and friendless. I am some tired. This here road is rough. That there man is homely. pshaw i am so Disgusted. Whoa can't you stand still. James the gardener gave me a white lily. Irving the genial writer lived on the hudson.

LESSON 67.
COMPOSITION.

Construct one sentence out of each group of the sentences which follow : —

Model. — An *able* man was chosen.
  A *prudent* man was chosen.
  An *honorable* man was chosen.

An *able, prudent,* and *honorable* man was chosen.

  Pure water is destitute of color.
  Pure water is destitute of taste.
  Pure water is destitute of smell.

  Cicero was the greatest orator of his age.
  Demosthenes was the greatest orator of his age.

  Daisies peeped up here.
  Daisies peeped up there.
  Daisies peeped up everywhere.

Expand each of the following sentences into three: —

The English language is spoken in England, Canada, and the United States. The Missouri, Ohio, and Arkansas rivers are branches of the Mississippi.

Out of the four following sentences compose one sentence having three explanatory modifiers : —

Model. — Elizabeth was *the daughter of Henry VIII.*
  Elizabeth was *sister of Queen Mary.*
  Elizabeth was the *patron of literature.*
  Elizabeth defeated the Armada.

Elizabeth, *the daughter of Henry VIII., sister of Queen Mary, and the patron of literature,* defeated the Armada.

Boston is the capital of Massachusetts.
Boston is the Athens of America.
Boston is the "Hub of the Universe."
Boston has crooked streets.

Expand the following sentence into four sentences:—

Daniel Webster, the great jurist, the expounder of the Constitution, and the chief of the "American Triumvirate," died with the words, "I still live," on his lips.

LESSON 68.

COMPOSITION.

Change the following simple sentences into complex sentences by expanding the phrases into adjective clauses:—

Model.—People *living in glass houses* shouldn't throw stones.
People *who live in glass houses* shouldn't throw stones.

Those living in the Arctic regions need much oily food.
A house built upon the rock will stand.
The boy of studious habits will always have his lesson.
Wellington was a man of iron will.
A scholar without money is not a bankrupt.
Everybody has something to teach us.
A race shortening its weapons extends its boundaries.

Change the following complex sentences into simple sentences by contracting the adjective clauses into phrases:—

Much of the cotton which is raised in the Gulf States is exported.
The house which was built upon the sand fell.
A thing which is beautiful is a joy forever.
Aaron Burr was a man who had fascinating manners.
Glaciers, which flow down mountain gorges, obey the law of rivers.
The best sermon which was ever preached on modern society is "Vanity Fair."
In mere love of what was vile, Charles II. surpassed all his subjects.
A common English ending is *er*, which is indicative of the agent.

Change the following simple sentences into complex sentences by expanding the phrases into adverb clauses: —

Model. — Birds return *in the spring; when spring comes*, the birds return.

The dog came at call. In old age our senses fail.
Shakespeare died at his birthplace.
Wishing to enjoy the Adirondacks, you must carry mountains in your brain.
Staying at home, one may visit Italy and the tropics.
Death, delaying his visits long, will certainly knock at every door.
A shrug of the shoulders, translated into words, would lose much.
Modern failures are of such magnitude as to appall the imagination.

Change the following complex sentences into simple sentences by contracting the adverb clauses into phrases: —

The ship started when the tide was at flood.
When he reached the middle of his speech, he stopped.
Error dies of lockjaw if she scratches her finger.
Some minute animals feed though they have no mouths.
Roads are built that travelers may be accommodated.
Shakespeare died where he was born

Supply noun clauses and make complete sentences out of the following expressions: —

—— is a well-known fact. The fact was ——. Ben Franklin said ——.

Contract the dependent clauses of these sentences into phrases: —

Arnold was fearful that he should be detected.
When one has eaten honey, one's tea seems to be without sugar.
Cairo is situated where the Ohio joins the Mississippi.
The effect of friction is, that it heats the substances rubbed.
He had no place where he might lay his head.
That we should defend ourselves is a duty.
If the farmer allows the weeds to grow unchecked, he will gather no harvest.
Mohammedans promise that they will obey the teachings of the Koran.
Dark clothes are warm in summer, because they absorb the rays of the sun.

LESSON 69.

GENERAL REVIEW.

What is a letter? Give the name and the sound of each of the letters in the three following words: *letters, name, sound.* Into what classes are letters divided? Define each class. Subdivide the consonants. Name the vowels. What is a word? What is verbal language? What is English Grammar? What is a sentence? What is the difference between the two expressions, *ripe apples* and *apples are ripe?* What two parts must every sentence have? Define each.

What is the analysis of a sentence? What is a diagram? What are parts of speech? How many parts of speech are there? Give an example of each. What is a noun? What is a verb? What must every predicate contain? What is a pronoun? What is a modifier? What is an adjective? What adjectives are sometimes called articles? When is *a* used? When is *an* used? Illustrate. Give an example of one modifier joined to another. What is an adverb? What is a phrase? A compound phrase? A complex? What is a preposition? What is a conjunction? What is an interjection? Give four rules for the use of capital letters (Lessons 8, 15, 19, 37). Give two rules for the use of the period, one for the exclamation point, and one for the interrogation point (Lessons 8, 37, 63).

LESSON 70.

GENERAL REVIEW.

What is an object complement? What is an attribute complement? How does a participle differ from a predicate verb? Illustrate. What offices does an infinitive phrase perform? Illustrate. How are sentences classified with respect to form? Give an example of each class. What is a simple sentence? What is a clause? What is a dependent clause? What is an independent clause? What is a complex sentence? What is a compound sentence? How are sentences classified with respect to meaning? Give an example of each class. What is a declarative sentence? What is an interrogative sentence? What is an imperative sentence? What is an exclamatory sentence? What different offices may a noun perform? *Ans.* — A noun may be used as a subject, as an object complement, as an attribute complement, as a possessive modifier, as an explanatory modifier, as the principal word in a prepositional phrase, and it may be used independently. Illustrate each use. What are sometimes substituted for nouns? *Ans.* — Pronouns, phrases, and clauses. Illustrate. What is the principal office of a verb? What offices may be performed by a phrase? What, by a clause? What different offices may an adjective perform? What parts of a speech may connect clauses? *Ans.* — Conjunctions, adverbs, and pronouns (Lessons 62, 59, and 57). Give rules for the use of the comma (Lessons 37, 54, 57). Give and illustrate the directions for using adjectives and adverbs, for placing phrases, for using prepositions, and for using negatives (Lessons 40, 41).

To the Teacher. — For additional review, see "Scheme," p. 267.

COMPOSITION OF SENTENCES AND OF PARAGRAPHS.

SELECTION FROM BEECHER.

Overwork almost always ends in weakening the digestive organs. There are those who overtax their minds through months and years, forgetful that there is a close connection between overwork and dyspepsia. Every one should remember that there is a point beyond which he cannot urge his brain without harm to his stomach; and that, when he loses his stomach, he loses the very citadel of health. The whole body is renewed from the blood, and the blood is made from the food taken into the stomach. The power of the blood to renew bone and brain and muscle depends upon a good digestion.

Too little sleep is fatal to health. Perhaps you have to work hard all day; but that is no reason why you should resolve, "If I cannot have pleasure by day, I will have it at night." You are taking the very substance of your body when you burn the lamp of pleasure till one or two o'clock in the morning. God has made sleep to be a sponge with which to rub out fatigue. A man's roots are planted in night, as a tree's are planted in soil, and out of it he should come, at waking, with fresh growth and bloom. As a rule, you should take eight hours of the twenty-four, for sleep.

The Uses of Words and Groups of Words. — In the exercises under the selection from the Brothers Grimm what did you learn about *there* as used twice in the second sentence above? What does *those* mean? What long adjective clause is joined to *those* by *who?* Does this clause read so closely as not to need a comma before *who?* Does *forgetful* describe the persons represented by *who?* Why is a comma used before *forgetful?* You learned in a preceding exercise that a noun may do the work of an adverb phrase without the help of a preposition. A noun clause may do the same. The adjective *forgetful* is modified by the noun clause, *that . . . dyspepsia.* If we say *forgetful of the fact,* we see that the noun clause means the same as *fact* and has the same office. What two long noun clauses are used to complete *should remember?* What conjunction introduces each of these clauses? What conjunction joins them together? What mark of punctuation between? If one of these noun clauses were not itself divided into clauses by the comma, would the semicolon be needed? The clause, *beyond . . . stomach,* goes with what word? *When . . . stomach* modifies what verb? Classify the sentences of this paragraph as simple, complex, or compound.

To the Teacher. — We have here treated informally some difficult points. Perhaps these may be better understood when the book is reviewed.

The Various Objects Writers Have. — From your study of the preceding selections you learn that a writer may have any one of several objects in writing. He may wish simply to instruct the reader, as does Darwin in what he says of earthworms. He may wish merely to amuse the reader, as does Mr. Habberton in our extract from "Helen's Babies." He may wish only to put before us a picture which, like that of George Eliot's, shall afford delight. Or he may wish to get hold of what we call our wills and lead us to do something, perform some duty. This is what the story from the Brothers Grimm aims at.

And you saw how it does this — by working on our feelings. There are at least these four objects that a writer may propose to himself. Which of these four objects has Mr. Beecher in the paragraphs we quote? Does he instruct? Does he try to get us to do something? Would it help you to have clearly before you from the beginning the object you are seeking to accomplish?

Figurative Expressions. — In these paragraphs Mr. Beecher calls a man's stomach the citadel of health, and sleep a sponge to rub out fatigue with, and says a man's roots are planted in night. He does not use these words *citadel, sponge,* and *roots* in their first or common meaning. He uses them in what we call a figurative sense. He means to say that a man's stomach is to him what a fortress is to soldiers, a source of strength; that in sleep fatigue disappears as do figures on a slate or blackboard when a wet sponge is drawn across them; and that a man gets out of night what a tree's roots draw out of the soil — nourishment and vigor. Such figurative uses of words give strength and beauty to style.

ORIGINAL COMPOSITION.

In the paragraphs quoted above, you were told of the effects on health of overwork and of insufficient sleep. Perhaps you can write of exercise, of proper food, of clothes, or of some other things on which health may depend.

To the Teacher. — If the early presentation of an outline of technical grammar is not compelled by a prescribed course of study, we should here introduce a series of lessons in the construction of sentences, paragraphs, and themes.

Here is an exercise in combining simple statements into complex and compound sentences, and in resolving complex and compound sentences into simple sentences. In combining statements, it is an excellent practice for the pupil to contract, expand, transpose, and to substitute other words. They thus learn to express the same thought in a variety of ways. Any reading-book or history will furnish good material for such practice.

Combine in as many ways as possible each of the following groups of sentences : —

Example. — This man is to be pitied. He has no friends.
1. This man has no friends, and he is to be pitied.
2. This man is to be pitied, because he has no friends.
3. Because this man has no friends, he is to be pitied.
4. This man, who has no friends, is to be pitied.
5. This man, having no friends, is to be pitied.
6. This man, without friends, is to be pitied.
7. This friendless man deserves our pity.

1. The ostrich is unable to fly. It has not wings in proportion to its body.

2. Egypt is a fertile country. It is annually inundated by the Nile.

3. The nerves are little threads, or fibers. They extend from the brain. They spread over the whole body.

4. John Gutenberg published a book. It was the first book known to have been printed on a printing-press. He was aided by the patronage of John Faust. He published it in 1455. He published it in the city of Mentz.

5. The human body is a machine. A watch is delicately constructed. This machine is more delicately constructed. A steam-engine is complicated. This machine is more complicated. A steam-engine is wonderful. This machine is more wonderful.

You see that short sentences closely related in meaning may be improved by being combined. But young writers frequently use too many *ands* and other connectives, and make their sentences too long.

Long sentences should be broken up into short ones when the relations of the parts are not clear.

As clauses may be joined to form sentences, so, as you have learned, sentences may be united to make paragraphs.

The first word of a paragraph should, as you have seen, begin a new line, and should be written a little farther to the right than the first words of other lines.

Combine the following statements into sentences and paragraphs, and make of them a complete composition, or theme: —

Water is a liquid. It is composed of oxygen and hydrogen. It covers about three-fourths of the surface of the earth. It takes the form of ice. It takes the form of snow. It takes the form of vapor. The air is constantly taking up water from rivers, lakes, oceans, and from damp ground. Cool air contains moisture. Heated air contains more moisture. Heated air becomes lighter. It rises. It becomes cool. The moisture is condensed into fine particles. Clouds are formed. They float across the sky. The little particles unite and form raindrops. They sprinkle the dry fields. At night the grass and flowers become cool. The air is not so cool. The warm air touches the grass and flowers. It is chilled. It loses a part of its moisture. Drops of dew are formed. Water has many uses. Men and animals drink it. Trees and plants drink it. They drink it by means of their leaves and roots. Water is a great purifier. It cleanses our bodies. It washes our clothes. It washes the dust from the leaves and the flowers. Water is a great worker. It floats vessels. It turns the wheels of mills. It is converted into steam. It is harnessed to mighty engines. It does the work of thousands of men and horses.

To the Teacher. — Condensed statements of facts, taken from some book not in the hands of your pupils, may be read to them, and they may be required to expand and combine these and group them into paragraphs.

PARTS OF SPEECH SUBDIVIDED.

LESSON 71.

CLASSES OF NOUNS.

Hints for Oral Instruction. — Hereafter, in the "Hints," we shall drop the dialogue form; but we expect the teacher to continue it. A poor teacher does all the talking, a good teacher makes the pupils talk.

The teacher may here refer to his talk about the classification of birds, and show that, after birds have been arranged in great classes, such as robins, sparrows, etc., these classes will need to be subdivided if the pupil is to be made thoroughly acquainted with this department of the animal kingdom. So, after grouping words into the eight great classes, called Parts of Speech, these classes may be divided into other classes. For instance, take the two nouns *city* and *Brooklyn*. The word *city* is the common name of all places of a certain class, but the word *Brooklyn* is the proper or particular name of an individual of this class. We have here then two kinds of nouns which we call **Common** and **Proper**.

Let the teacher write a number of nouns on the board,

and require the pupil to classify them and give the reasons for the classification.

To prepare the pupil thoroughly for this work, the teacher will find it necessary to explain why such words as *music, mathematics, knowledge,* etc. are common nouns. *Music,* e.g., is not a proper noun, for it is not a name given to an individual thing to distinguish it from other things of the same class. There are no other things of the same class — it forms a class by itself. So we call the noun *music* a common noun.

CLASSES OF PRONOUNS.

The speaker seldom refers to himself by name, but uses the pronoun *I* instead. In speaking to a person, we often use the pronoun *you* instead of his name. In speaking of a person or thing that has been mentioned before, we say *he* or *she* or *it*. These words that by their form indicate the speaker, the hearer, or the person or thing spoken of are called **Personal Pronouns** (Lesson 19).

Give sentences containing nouns repeated, and require the pupils to improve these sentences by substituting pronouns.

When we wish to refer to an object that has been mentioned in another clause, and at the same time to connect the clauses, we use a class of pronouns called **Relative Pronouns**. Let the teacher illustrate by using the pronouns *who, which,* and *that* (Lesson 57).

When we wish to ask about anything whose name is unknown, we use a class of pronouns called **Interrogative Pronouns.** The interrogative pronoun stands for the unknown name and asks for it; as, "*Who* comes here?" "*What* is this?"

"*Both men* were wrong." Let us omit *men* and say, "*Both* were wrong." You see the meaning is not changed — *both* is here equivalent to *both men*, that is, it performs the office of an adjective and that of a noun. It is therefore an **Adjective Pronoun.** Let the teacher further illustrate the office of the adjective pronoun by using the words *each, all, many, some, such,* etc.

DEFINITIONS.

CLASSES OF NOUNS.

A **Common Noun** is a name which belongs to all things of a class.

A **Proper Noun** is the particular name of an individual.

CLASSES OF PRONOUNS.

A **Personal Pronoun** is a pronoun that by its form denotes the speaker, the one spoken to, or the one spoken of.

A **Relative Pronoun** is one that relates to some preceding word or words and connects clauses.

An **Interrogative Pronoun** is one with which a question is asked.

An **Adjective Pronoun** is one that performs the offices of both an adjective and a noun.

LESSON 72.

COMPOSITION.

Build each of the following groups of nouns into a sentence. See Rule, Lesson 15.

webster cares office washington repose home marshfield.

george washington commander army revolution president united states westmoreland state virginia month february.

san francisco city port pacific trade united states lines steamships sandwich islands japan china australia.

Write five simple sentences, each containing one of the five personal pronouns: *I, thou* or *you, he, she*, and *it*.

Write four complex sentences, each containing one of the four relative pronouns: *who, which, that,* and *what*.

What is used as a relative pronoun when the antecedent is omitted. The word for which a pronoun stands is called its **Antecedent**. When we express the antecedent, we use *which* or *that*. "I shall do *what* is required;" "I shall do the *thing which* is required, or *that* is required."

Build three interrogative sentences, each containing one of the three interrogative pronouns *who, which*, and *what*.

Build eight sentences, each containing one of the adjective pronouns *few, many, much, some, this, these, that, those.*

LESSON 73.

CLASSES OF ADJECTIVES.

Hints for Oral Instruction.—When I say *large, round, sweet, yellow oranges*, the words *large, round, sweet,* and *yellow* modify the word *oranges* by telling the kind, and limit the application of the word to oranges of that kind.

When I say *this orange, yonder orange, one orange*, the words *this, yonder,* and *one* do not tell the kind, but simply point out or number the orange, and limit the application of the word to the orange pointed out or numbered.

Adjectives of the first class describe by giving a quality, and so are called **Descriptive Adjectives.**

Adjectives of the second class define by pointing out or numbering, and so are called **Definitive Adjectives.**

Let the teacher write nouns on the board, and require the pupils to modify them by appropriate descriptive and definitive adjectives.

DEFINITIONS.

A **Descriptive Adjective** is one that modifies by expressing quality.

A **Definitive Adjective** is one that modifies by pointing out, numbering, or denoting quantity.

COMPOSITION.

Place the following adjectives in two columns, one headed descriptive and the other definitive, then build simple sentences in which they shall be employed as modifiers. Find out the meaning of each word before you use it: —

Round, frolicsome, first, industrious, jolly, idle, skillful, each, the, faithful, an, kind, one, tall, ancient, modern, dancing, mischievous, stationary, nimble, several, slanting, parallel, oval, every.

Build simple sentences in which the following descriptive adjectives shall be employed as attribute complements. Let some of these attributes be compound: —

Restless, impulsive, dense, rare, gritty, sluggish, dingy, selfish, clear, cold, sparkling, slender, graceful, hungry, friendless.

Build simple sentences in which the following descriptive adjectives shall be employed. Some of these adjectives have the form of participles, and others are derived from proper nouns: —

Shining, moving, swaying, bubbling, American, German, French, Swiss, Irish, Chinese.

CAPITAL LETTER — RULE. — An Adjective derived from a proper noun must begin with a capital letter.

LESSON 74.

CLASSES OF VERBS.

Hints for Oral Instruction. — "The man *caught*" makes no complete assertion and is not a sentence. If we add the object complement *fish*, we complete the assertion and form a sentence—"The man *caught fish*." The action expressed by *caught* passes over from the man to the fish. *Transitive* means passing over, and hence all those verbs that express an action that passes over from the doer to something which receives are called **Transitive Verbs.**

"Fish *swim*." The verb *swim* does not require an object to complete the sentence. No action passes from a doer to a receiver. These verbs which express action that does not pass over to a receiver, and all those which do not express action at all, but simply being or state of being, are called **Intransitive Verbs.**

Let the teacher write transitive and intransitive verbs on the board, and require the pupils to distinguish them.

When I say, "I *crush* the worm," I express an action that is going on now, or in present time. "I *crushed* the worm," expresses an action that took place in past time. As *tense* means time, we call the form *crush* the present tense of the verb, and *crushed* the past tense. In the sentence, "The worm *crushed* under my foot died," *crushed*, expressing the action as assumed, is, as you have already learned, a participle; and, as the action is completed, we call it a past participle. Now notice that ed was added to *crush*, the verb in the present tense, to form the verb in the past tense, and to form the past participle. Most verbs form their past tense and their past participle by adding ed, and so we call such **Regular Verbs.**

"I *see* the man;" "I *saw* the man;" "The man *seen*

by me ran away." "I *catch* fish in the brook;" "I *caught* fish in the brook;" "The fish *caught* in the brook tasted good." Here the verbs *see* and *catch* do not form their past tense and past participle by adding **ed** to the present, and hence we call them **Irregular Verbs**.

Let the teacher write on the board verbs of both classes, and require the pupils to distinguish them.

DEFINITIONS.

CLASSES OF VERBS WITH RESPECT TO MEANING.

A **Transitive Verb** is one that requires an object.[1]

An **Intransitive Verb** is one that does not require an object.

CLASSES OF VERBS WITH RESPECT TO FORM.

A **Regular Verb** is one that forms its past tense and past participle by adding **ed** to the present.[2]

---

[1] The object of a transitive verb, that is, the name of the receiver of the action, may be the object complement, or it may be the subject; as, "Brutus stabbed *Cæsar*," "*Cæsar* was stabbed by Brutus."

[2] If the present ends in e, the e is dropped when **ed** is added; as love, loved; believe, believed.

It is quite common to classify verbs as **weak** and **strong** rather than as regular and irregular. Weak verbs are those that form their past tense by adding **ed** — or some form of it, as **d** or **t** — to the present; strong verbs are those that form their past tense by **vowel-change** alone. The full ending of the past participle weak is **ed**, and of the past participle strong is **en**.

Regular and irregular, if used, would denote those verbs that (1) **do**, and those that (2) **do not**, conform perfectly to the two types. *Fall, fell,*

An **Irregular Verb** is one that does not form its past tense and past participle by adding ed to the present.

COMPOSITION.

Place the following verbs in two columns, one headed transitive and the other intransitive. Place the same verbs in two other columns, one headed regular and the other irregular. Build these verbs into sentences by supplying a subject to each intransitive verb, and a subject and an object to each transitive verb:—

Vanish, gallop, bite, promote, contain, produce, provide, veto, secure, scramble, rattle, draw.

Arrange the following verbs as before, and then build them into sentences by supplying a subject and a noun attribute to each intransitive verb, and a subject and an object to each transitive verb:—

Degrade, gather, know, was, became, is.

A verb may be transitive in one sentence and intransitive in another. Use the following verbs both ways:—

Model.—The wren *sings* sweetly.
The wren *sings* a pretty little song.

Bend, ring, break, dash, move.

fallen would be a regular strong verb; and *walk, walked, walked*, a regular weak verb. *Wear, wore, worn*, would be an irregular strong verb; and *creep, crept, crept*, an irregular weak verb.

LESSON 75.
CLASSES OF ADVERBS.

Hints for Oral Instruction. — When I say, "He will come *soon*, or *presently*, or *often*, or *early*," I am using, to modify *will come*, words which express the time of coming. These and all such adverbs we call **Adverbs of Time**.

"He will come *up*, or *hither*, or *here*, or *back*." Here I use, to modify *will come*, words which express place. These and all such adverbs we call **Adverbs of Place**.

When I say, "The weather is *so* cold, or *very* cold, or *intensely* cold," the words *so*, *very*, and *intensely* modify the adjective *cold* by expressing the degree of coldness. These and all such adverbs we call **Adverbs of Degree**.

When I say, "He spoke *freely*, *wisely*, and *well*," the words *freely*, *wisely*, and *well* tell how or in what manner he spoke. All such adverbs we call **Adverbs of Manner**.

Let the teacher place adverbs on the board, and require the pupil to classify them.

DEFINITIONS.

Adverbs of Time are those that generally answer the question, *When?*

Adverbs of Place are those that generally answer the question, *Where?*

Adverbs of Degree are those that generally answer the question, *To what extent?*

Adverbs of Manner are those that generally answer the question, *In what way?*

COMPOSITION.

Place the following adverbs in the four classes we have made — if the classification be perfect, there will be five words in each column — then build each adverb into a simple sentence: —

Partly, only, too, wisely, now, here, when, very, well, where, nobly, already, seldom, more, ably, away, always, not, there, out.

Some adverbs, as you have already learned, modify two verbs, and thus connect the two clauses in which these verbs occur. Such adverbs are called **Conjunctive Adverbs.**

The following dependent clauses are introduced by conjunctive adverbs. Build them into complex sentences by supplying independent clauses: —

—— *when* the ice is smooth ; —— *while* we sleep ; —— *before* winter comes ; —— *where* the reindeer lives ; —— *wherever* you go.

LESSON 76.
CLASSES OF CONJUNCTIONS.

Hints for Oral Instruction. — "*Frogs, antelopes, and kangaroos* can jump." Here the three nouns are of the same rank in the sentence. All are subjects of *can jump*. "*War has ceased, and peace has come.*" In this compound sentence, there are two clauses of the same rank. The word *and* connects the subjects of *can jump*, in the first sentence; and the two clauses, in the second. All words that connect words, phrases, or clauses of the same rank are called **Coördinate Conjunctions.**

"*If you have tears, prepare to shed them now;*" "*I will go, because you need me.*" Here *if* joins the clause, *you have tears,* as a modifier expressing condition, to the independent clause, "*prepare to shed them now*"; and *because* connects "*you need me,*" as a modifier expressing reason or cause, to the independent clause, "*I will go.*" These and all such conjunctions as connect dependent clauses to clauses of a higher rank are called **Subordinate Conjunctions.**

Let the teacher illustrate the meaning and use of the words *subordinate* and *coördinate.*

DEFINITIONS.

Coördinate Conjunctions are such as connect words, phrases, or clauses of the same rank.

Subordinate Conjunctions are such as connect clauses of different rank.

COMPOSITION.

Build four short sentences for each of the three coördinate conjunctions that follow. In the first, let the conjunction be used to connect principal parts of a sentence; in the second, to connect word modifiers; in the third, to connect phrase modifiers; and in the fourth, to connect independent clauses: —

And, or, but.

Write four short complex sentences containing the four subordinate conjunctions that follow. Let the first be used to introduce a noun clause, and the others to connect adverb clauses to independent clauses: —

That, for, if, because.

LIST OF CONNECTIVES.

Remark. — Some of the connectives below are conjunctions proper; some are relative pronouns; and some are adverbs or adverb phrases, which, in addition to their office as modifiers, may, in the absence of the conjunction, take its office upon themselves and connect the clauses.

COÖRDINATE CONNECTIVES.

Copulative. — *And, both* . . . *and, as well as*[1] are conjunctions proper. *Accordingly, also, besides, consequently, furthermore, hence, likewise, moreover, now, so, then,* and *therefore* are conjunctive adverbs.

Adversative. — *But* and *whereas* are conjunctions proper. *However, nevertheless, notwithstanding, on the contrary, on the other hand, still,* and *yet* are conjunctive adverbs.

Alternative. — *Neither, nor, or, either* . . . *or,* and *neither* . . . *nor* are conjunctions proper. *Else* and *otherwise* are conjunctive adverbs.

SUBORDINATE CONNECTIVES.

CONNECTIVES OF ADJECTIVE CLAUSES.

That, what, whatever, which, whichever, who, and *whoever* are relative pronouns. *When, where, whereby, wherein,* and *why* are conjunctive adverbs.

---

[1] The *as well as* in " He, *as well as* I, went"; and not that in " He is *as well as* I am."

CONNECTIVES OF ADVERB CLAUSES.

Time. — *After, as, before, ere, since, till, until, when, whenever, while,* and *whilst* are conjunctive adverbs.

Place. — *Whence, where,* and *wherever* are conjunctive adverbs.

Degree. — *As, than, that,* and *the* are conjunctive adverbs, correlative with adjectives or adverbs.

Manner. — *As* is a conjunctive adverb, correlative often with an adjective or an adverb.

Real Cause. — *As, because, for, since,* and *whereas* are conjunctions proper.

Evidence. — *Because, for,* and *since* are conjunctions proper.

Purpose. — *In order that, lest* (= *that not*), *that,* and *so that* are conjunctions proper.

Condition. — *Except, if, in case that, on condition that, provided, provided that,* and *unless* are conjunctions proper.

Concession. — *Although, if* (= *even if*), *notwithstanding, though,* and *whether* are conjunctions proper. *However* is a conjunctive adverb. *Whatever, whichever,* and *whoever* are relative pronouns used indefinitely.

CONNECTIVES OF NOUN CLAUSES.

If, lest, that, and *whether* are conjunctions proper. *What, which,* and *who* are pronouns introducing questions; *how, when, whence, where,* and *why* are conjunctive adverbs.

LESSON 77.
REVIEW QUESTIONS.

What new subject begins with Lesson 74? Name and define the different classes of nouns. Illustrate by examples the difference between common nouns and proper nouns. Name and define the different classes of pronouns. Can the pronoun *I* be used to stand for the one spoken to? — the one spoken of? Does the relative pronoun distinguish by its form the speaker, the one spoken to, and the one spoken of? Illustrate. What office is performed by a relative pronoun besides that of representing some antecedent noun or pronoun? Illustrate. Can any other class of pronouns be used to connect clauses?

For what do interrogative pronouns stand? Illustrate. Where may the antecedent of an interrogative pronoun generally be found? *Ans.* — The antecedent of an interrogative pronoun may generally be found in the answer to the question.

Name and define the different classes of adjectives. Give an example of each class. Name and define the different classes of verbs, made with respect to their meaning. Give an example of each class. Name and define the different classes of verbs, made with respect to their form. Give an example of each class.

Name and define the different classes of adverbs. Give examples of each kind. Name and define the different classes of conjunctions. Illustrate by examples.

Are prepositions and interjections subdivided? (See "Schemes" for the conjunction, the preposition, and the interjection, p. 270.)

COMPOSITION OF SENTENCES AND OF PARAGRAPHS.

ADAPTED FROM DR. JOHN BROWN — "RAB AND HIS FRIENDS."

Rab belonged to a lost tribe — there are no such dogs now. He was old and gray and brindled; and his hair short, hard, and close, like a lion's. He was as big as a Highland bull, and his body was thickset. He must have weighed ninety pounds at least.

His large, blunt head was scarred with the record of old wounds, a series of battlefields all over it. His muzzle was as black as night, his mouth blacker than any night, and a tooth or two, all he had, gleamed out of his jaws of darkness. One eye was out, one ear cropped close. The remaining eye had the power of two; and above it, and in constant communication with it, was a tattered rag of an ear that was forever unfurling itself like an old flag.

And then that bud of a tail, about an inch long, if it could in any sense be said to be long, being as broad as it was long! The mobility of it, its expressive twinklings and winkings, and the intercommunications between the eye, the ear, and it were of the oddest and swiftest.

Rab had the dignity and simplicity of great size. Having fought his way all along the road to absolute supremacy, he was as mighty in his own line as Julius Cæsar or the Duke of Wellington in his, and he had the gravity of all great fighters.

To the Teacher. — On the uses of words we suggest exercises similar to those preceding. Before attempting this it may be well to let the pupils go over these condensed expressions and supply the words necessary to the analysis. For instance, in the first paragraph *hair* may be followed by *was* and *Highland bull* by *is big*. In the next paragraph *wounds* may be followed by *marking, as night* by *is black*, etc. In the third paragraph *and then* may be followed by *there was*, etc. The pupils will determine whether supplying these words makes the description stronger or weaker.

Pupils may note especially the offices of nouns, verbs, and adjectives. This selection abounds in descriptive nouns and verbs that are particularly well chosen. Let the pupils point out such.

The Description. — How does the description above impress you? Are only characteristic parts and features selected? Are these few features enough to give you a distinct and vivid picture of Rab? What comparisons do you find? How do they help? Pick out some words or phrases that seem to you very expressive. Find some words that are used, not in their first or common sense, but in a figurative sense. How do they help?

Paragraphs. — Which paragraph puts before you the dog as a whole? Where must this paragraph naturally stand? Why? Which paragraph describes Rab's character? What does each of the other paragraphs describe? If you think the arrangement of paragraphs above is the best, tell why.

Make a framework for this description.

ORIGINAL COMPOSITION.

Write a description of some animal which you have closely observed and in which you are interested. Be careful to pick out leading or characteristic features that will bring others into the reader's imagination. First prepare a framework.

REVIEW — COMPOSITION.

We recommend that the teacher select some short article containing valuable information and break up each paragraph into short, disconnected expressions. One paragraph at a time may be put on the board for the pupils to copy. The general subject may be given, and the pupils may be required to find a proper heading for the paragraph. The different ways of connecting the expressions may be discussed in the class. By contracting, expanding, and transposing, and by substituting entirely different words, a great variety of forms may be had. (The list of connectives in Lesson 76 may be helpful.) The pupils may then combine the different paragraphs into a composition.

We give, below, material for one composition, or theme: —

Frog's spawn found in a pond. At first like a mass of jelly. Eggs can be distinguished.

In a few days curious little fish are hatched. These "tadpoles" are lively. Swim by means of long tails. Head very large — out of proportion. Appearance of all head and tail. This creature is a true fish. It breathes water-air by means of gills. It has a two-chambered heart.

Watch it day by day. Two little gills seen. These soon disappear. Hind legs begin to grow. Tail gets smaller. Two small arms, or forelegs, are seen. Remarkable change going on inside. True lungs for breathing air have been forming. Another chamber added to the heart.

As the gills grow smaller, it finds difficulty in breathing water-air. One fine day it pokes its nose out of the water. Astonished (possibly) to find that it can breathe in the air. A new life has come upon it. No particular reason for spending all its time in water; crawls out upon land; sits down upon its haunches; surveys the world. It is no longer a fish; has entered upon a higher stage of existence; has become a frog.

This work of analyzing a composition to find the leading thoughts under which the other thoughts may be grouped is in many ways a most valuable discipline.

It teaches the pupil to compare, to discriminate, to weigh, to systematize, to read intelligently and profitably.

The reading-book will afford excellent practice in finding heads for paragraphs. Such work is an essential preparation for the reading class.

This composition work should serve as a constant review of all that has been passed over in the text-book

MODIFICATIONS OF THE PARTS OF SPEECH.

LESSON 78.

NOUNS AND PRONOUNS.

Hints for Oral Instruction. — You have learned that two words may express a thought, and that the thought may be varied by adding modifying words. You are now to learn that the meaning or use of a word may sometimes be changed by simply changing its form. The English language has lost many of its inflections, or forms, so that frequently changes in the meaning and use of words are not marked by changes in form. These changes in the form, meaning, and use of the parts of speech we call their **Modifications**.

"The *boy* shouts;" "The *boys* shout." I have changed the form of the subject *boy* by adding an **s** to it. The meaning has changed. *Boy* denotes one lad; *boys*, two or more lads. This change in the form and meaning of nouns is called **Number**. The word *boy*, denoting one thing, is in the **Singular Number**; and *boys*, denoting more than one thing, is in the **Plural Number**.

Let the teacher write other nouns on the board, and require the pupils to form the plural of them.

DEFINITIONS.

Modifications of the Parts of Speech are changes in their form, meaning, and use.

NUMBER.

Number is that modification of a noun or pronoun which denotes one thing or more than one.

The **Singular Number** denotes one thing.

The **Plural Number** denotes more than one thing.

RULE. — The **plural** of nouns is regularly formed by adding *s* or *es* to the singular.

Write the plural of the following nouns : —

Tree, bird, insect, cricket, grasshopper, wing, stick, stone, flower, meadow, pasture, grove, worm, bug, cow, eagle, hawk, wren, plow, shovel.

When a singular noun ends in the sound of **s, x, z, sh**, or **ch**, it is not easy to add the sound of **s**, so **es** is added to make another syllable.

Write the plural of the following nouns : —

Guess, box, topaz, lash, birch, compass, fox, waltz, sash, bench, gas, tax, adz, brush, arch.

Many nouns ending in **o** preceded by a consonant form the plural by adding **es** without increasing the number of syllables.

Nouns and Pronouns.—Number.

Write the plural of the following nouns : —

Hero, cargo, negro, potato, echo, volcano, mosquito, motto.

Common nouns ending in **y** preceded by a consonant form the plural by changing **y** into **i** and adding **es** without increasing the number of syllables.

Write the plural of the following nouns : —

Lady, balcony, family, city, country, daisy, fairy, cherry, study, sky.

Some nouns ending in **f** and **fe** form the plural by changing **f** or **fe** into **ves** without increasing the number of syllables.

Write the plural of the following nouns : —

Sheaf, loaf, beef, thief, calf, half, elf, shelf, self, wolf, life, knife, wife.

LESSON 79.

NUMBER.

From the following list of nouns, select and write in separate columns (1) those that have no plural; (2) those that have no singular; (3) those that are alike in both numbers : —

Pride, wages, trousers, cider, suds, victuals, milk, riches, flax, courage, sheep, deer, flour, idleness, tidings, thanks, ashes, scissors, swine, heathen.

The following nouns have very irregular plurals — six changing the internal vowel, and two adding en. Learn to spell the plurals : —

Singular.	Plural.	Singular.	Plural.
Man,	men.	Foot,	feet.
Louse,	lice.	Ox,	oxen.
Child,	children.	Tooth,	teeth.
Mouse,	mice.	Goose,	geese.

Learn the following plurals and compare them with the groups in the preceding Lesson: —

Moneys, flies, chimneys, valleys, stories, berries, lilies, turkeys, monkeys, cuckoos, pianos, vetoes, solos, folios, gulfs, chiefs, leaves, roofs, scarfs, inches.

LESSON 80.
NOUNS AND PRONOUNS.—GENDER.

Hints for Oral Instruction. — " The *lion* was caged ; " " The *lioness* was caged." In the first sentence, something is said about a male lion ; and in the second, something is said about a female lion. Modifications of the noun to denote the sex of the object we call **Gender**. Knowing the sex of the object, you know the gender of its English name. The word *lion*, denoting a male animal, is in the **Masculine Gender** ; and *lioness*, denoting a female lion, is in the **Feminine Gender**.

The names of things without sex are in the **Neuter Gender**.

Such words as *cousin, child, friend, neighbor* may be either masculine or feminine.

DEFINITIONS.

Gender is that modification of a noun or pronoun which denotes sex.

The **Masculine Gender** denotes the male sex.
The **Feminine Gender** denotes the female sex.
The **Neuter Gender** denotes want of sex.

The feminine is distinguished from the masculine in three ways: —

(1) By a difference in the ending of the nouns.
(2) By different words in the compound names.
(3) By words wholly or radically different.

Arrange the following pairs in separate columns with reference to these ways: —

Abbot, abbess; actor, actress; Francis, Frances; Jesse, Jessie; bachelor, maid; beau, belle; monk, nun; gander, goose; administrator, administratrix; baron, baroness; count, countess; czar, czarina; don, donna; boy, girl; drake, duck; lord, lady; nephew, niece; landlord, landlady; gentleman, gentlewoman; peacock, peahen; duke, duchess; hero, heroine; host, hostess; Jew, Jewess; man-servant, maid-servant; sir, madam; wizard, witch; marquis, marchioness; widower, widow; heir, heiress; Paul, Pauline; Augustus, Augusta.

REVIEW QUESTIONS.

What new way of varying the meaning of words is introduced in Lesson 78? Illustrate. What are modifications of the parts of speech? What is number? How many numbers are there? Name and define each. Give the rule for forming the plural of nouns. Illustrate the variations of this rule. What is gender? How many genders are there? Name and define each. In how many ways are the genders distinguished? Illustrate.

LESSON 81.
NOUNS AND PRONOUNS. — PERSON AND CASE.

Hints for Oral Instruction. — Number and gender, as you have already learned, are modifications affecting the meaning of nouns and pronouns. Number is almost always indicated by the ending; gender, sometimes. There are two other modifications which refer not to changes in the meaning of nouns and pronouns but to their different uses and relations. In the English language, these changes are not often indicated by a change of form.

"*I Paul* have written;" "*Paul, thou* art beside thyself;" "*He* brought *Paul* before Agrippa." In these three sentences the word *Paul* has three different uses. In the first, it is used as the name of the speaker; in the second, as the name of one spoken to; in the third, as the name of one spoken of. You will notice that the form of the noun is not changed. This change in the use of nouns and pronouns is called **Person**. The word *I* in the first sentence, the word *thou* in the second, and the word *he* in the third have each a different use. *I, thou*, and *he* are personal pronouns, and, as you have learned, distinguish person by their form. *I*, denoting the speaker, is in the **First Person**; *thou,* denoting the one spoken to, is in the **Second Person**; and *he,* denoting the one spoken of, is in the **Third Person.**

Personal pronouns and verbs are the only words that distinguish person by their form.

"The *bear killed* the *man;*" "The *man killed* the *bear;*" "The *bear's grease* was made into hair oil." In the first sentence, the bear is represented as performing an action; in the second, as receiving an action; in the third, as possessing something. Hence the word *bear* in these sentences has three different uses. These uses of nouns are called **Cases.** The use of a noun as subject is called the **Nominative Case**; its use as object is called the **Objective Case**; and its use to denote possession is called the **Possessive Case.**

The possessive is the only case of nouns that is indicated by a change in form.

A noun or pronoun used as an attribute complement is in the nominative case. A noun or pronoun following a preposition as the principal word of a phrase is in the objective case. *I* and *he* are nominative forms. *Me* and *him* are objective forms.

The following sentences are therefore incorrect: It is *me;* It is *him;* *Me* gave the pen to *he.*

DEFINITIONS.

Person is that modification of a noun or pronoun which denotes the speaker. the one spoken to, or the one spoken of.

The **First Person** denotes the one speaking.
The **Second Person** denotes the one spoken to.
The **Third Person** denotes the one spoken of.

Case is that modification of a noun or pronoun which denotes its office in the sentence.

The **Nominative Case** of a noun or pronoun denotes its office as subject or as attribute complement.

The **Possessive Case** of a noun or pronoun denotes its office as possessive modifier.

The **Objective Case** of a noun or pronoun denotes its office as object complement, or as principal word in a prepositional phrase.

LESSON 82.

NOUNS AND PRONOUNS.—PERSON AND CASE.

Tell the person and case of each of the following nouns and pronouns — **remembering** that a noun or pronoun used as an explanatory modifier is in the same case as the word which it explains, and that a noun or pronoun used independently is in the nominative case : —

We Americans do things in a hurry.
You Englishmen take more time to think.
The Germans do their work with the most patience and deliberation.
We boys desire a holiday.
Come on, my men; I will lead you.
I, your teacher, desire your success.

You, my pupils, are attentive.
I called on Tom, the tinker.
Friends, countrymen, and lovers, hear me for my cause.

Write simple sentences in which each of the following nouns shall be used in the three persons and in the three cases : —

Andrew Jackson, Alexander, Yankees.

Write a sentence containing a noun in the nominative case, used as an attribute; one in the nominative, used as an explanatory modifier; one in the nominative, used independently.

Write a sentence containing a noun in the objective case, used to complete two predicate verbs; one used to complete a participle; one used to complete an infinitive; one used with a preposition to make a phrase : one used as an explanatory modifier.

If the class is sufficiently mature, the objective complement may here be treated. This explanation may be of service : —

In " It made him *sad*," made does not fully express the action performed upon him — not " *made him*," but " *made sad* (saddened) *him.*" *Sad* helps *made* to express the action, and also denotes a quality which, as the result of the action, belongs to the person represented by the object *him*.

Whatever completes the predicate and belongs to the object we call an **Objective Complement.**

Nouns, infinitives, and participles may be used in the same way, as: —

They made Victoria *queen;*
It made him *weep;*
It kept him *laughing.*

They | made / queen | Victoria   Explanation. — The line that separates *made* from *queen* slants toward the object complement to show that *queen* belongs to the object.

A noun or pronoun used as objective complement is in the objective case.

The teacher may here explain such constructions as " I proved it to be *him*," in which *it* is object complement and *to be him* is objective complement. *Him*, the attribute complement of *be*, is in the objective case, because *it*, the assumed subject of *be*, is objective. Let the pupils compare, " I proved it to be *him* " with " I proved that it was *he*"; " *Whom* did you suppose it to be?" with " *Who* did you suppose it was?" etc.

These uses of nouns and pronouns may here be introduced, if the class be sufficiently mature: —

1. He gave *John* a book.   2. He bought *me* a book.

John and *me*, as here used, are called **Indirect Objects.** The indirect object names the one to or for whom something is done. We treat these words as modifiers without the preposition. If we change the order, the preposition must be supplied; as, " He gave a book *to John;*" " He bought a book *for me.*"

Nouns denoting measure, quantity, weight, time, value, distance, or direction may be used adverbially, being equivalent to phrase modifiers without the preposition, as : —

1. We walked four *miles* an *hour*.
2. It weighs one *pound*.
3. It is worth a *dollar*.
4. The wall is ten *feet* six *inches* high.
5. I went *home* that *way*.

The following diagram will illustrate both the **indirect object** and the **noun of measure** : —

They offered Cæsar the crown three times.

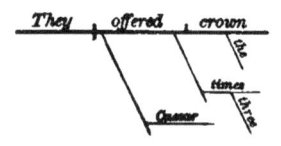

Explanation. — *Cæsar* (the indirect object) and *times* (denoting measure) stand in the diagram on lines representing the principal words of prepositional phrases.

LESSON 83.

NOUNS AND PRONOUNS. — DECLENSION.

DEFINITION. — **Declension** is the arrangement of the cases of nouns and pronouns in the two numbers.

DECLENSION OF NOUNS.

	LADY.		CHILD.	
	Singular.	*Plural.*	*Singular.*	*Plural.*
Nom.	lady,	ladies,	child,	children,
Pos.	lady's,	ladies',	child's,	children's,
Obj.	lady ;	ladies.	child ;	children.

Declension of Pronouns.

Personal Pronouns.

First Person.

	Singular.	Plural.
Nom.	I,	we,
Pos.	my *or* mine,	our *or* ours,
Obj.	me;	us.

Second Person — common form.

	Singular.	Plural.
Nom.	you,	you,
Pos.	your *or* yours,	your *or* yours,
Obj.	you;	you.

Second Person — old form.

	Singular.	Plural.
Nom.	thou,	ye *or* you,
Pos.	thy *or* thine,	your *or* yours,
Obj.	thee;	you.

Third Person — masculine.

	Singular.	Plural.
Nom.	he,	they,
Pos.	his,	their *or* theirs,
Obj.	him;	them.

Third Person — feminine.

	Singular.	Plural.
Nom.	she,	they,
Pos.	her *or* hers,	their *or* theirs,
Obj.	her;	them.

THIRD PERSON — neuter.

Singular.	Plural.
Nom. it,	they,
Pos. its,	their *or* theirs,
Obj. it;	them.

Mine, ours, yours, thine, hers, and *theirs* are used when the name of the thing possessed is omitted; as, "This rose is *yours*" = "This rose is *your rose.*"

COMPOUND PERSONAL PRONOUNS.

By joining the word *self* to the possessive forms *my, thy, your* and to the objective forms *him, her, it,* the **Compound Personal Pronouns** are formed. They have no possessive case, and are alike in the nominative and the objective.

Their plurals are *ourselves, yourselves,* and *themselves.* Form the compound personal pronouns, and write their declension.

RELATIVE AND INTERROGATIVE PRONOUNS.

Sing. and Plu.	Sing. and Plu.
Nom. who,	*Nom.* which,
Pos. whose,	*Pos.* whose,
Obj. whom.	*Obj.* which.

Of which is often used instead of the possessive form of the latter pronoun. In actual use, *whose,* interrogative, is the possessive of *who* only.

Sing. and Plu.   *Sing. and Plu.*
Nom. that,   *Nom.* what,
Pos. ——,   *Pos.* ——,
Obj. that.   *Obj.* what.

Ever and *soever* are added to *who*, *which*, and *what* to form the **Compound Relative Pronouns**. They are used when the antecedent is omitted. For declension see above.

LESSON 84.

POSSESSIVE FORMS.

RULE.—The **possessive case** of nouns is formed in the singular by adding to the nominative the apostrophe and the letter s ('s); in the plural, by adding the apostrophe (') only. If the plural does not end in s, the apostrophe and the s are both added.

Write the possessive singular and the possessive plural of the following nouns, and place an appropriate noun after each:—

Robin, friend, fly, hero, woman, bee, mouse, cuckoo, fox, ox, man, thief, fairy, mosquito, wolf, shepherd, farmer, child, neighbor, cow.

Possession may be expressed also by the preposition *of* and the objective; as, the *mosquito's* bill = the bill *of* the *mosquito*.

The possessive sign ('s) is confined chiefly to the names of persons and animals.

We do not say the *chair's* legs, but the legs *of* the *chair*. Regard must be had also to the sound.

Improve the following expressions, and expand each into a simple sentence: —

The sky's color; the cloud's brilliancy; the rose's leaves; my uncle's partner's house; George's father's friend's farm; the mane of the horse of my brother; my brother's horse's mane.

When there are several possessive nouns, all belonging to one word, the possessive sign is added to the last only. If they modify different words, the sign is added to each.

Correct the following expressions, and expand each into a simple sentence: —

Model. — *Webster and Worcester's* dictionary may be bought at *Ticknor's and Field's* bookstore.

The possessive sign should be added to *Webster*, for the word *dictionary* is understood immediately after. Webster and Worcester did not together possess the same dictionary. The sign should not be added to *Ticknor*, for the two men, Ticknor and Field, owned the same store.

Adam's and Eve's garden; Jacob's and Esau's father; Shakespeare and Milton's works; Maud, Kate, and Clara's gloves; Maud's. Kate's, and Clara's teacher was ———.

When one possessive noun is explanatory of another, the possessive sign is added to the last only.

Correct the following errors : —

I called at Tom's the tinker's. They listened to Peter's the Hermit's eloquence. This was the Apostle's Paul's advice.

Correct the following errors : —

Our's, your's, hi's, their's, her's, it's, hisn, yourn, hern.

LESSON 85.

FORMS OF THE PRONOUN.

Remember that *I, we, thou, ye, he, she, they,* and *who* are **nominative** forms, and must not be used in the objective case.

Remember that *me, us, thee, him, her, them,* and *whom* are **objective** forms, and must not be used in the nominative case.

To the Teacher. — The eight nominative forms and the seven objective forms given above are the only distinctive nominative and objective forms in the English language. Let the pupils become familiar with them.

Correct the following errors : —

Him and me are good friends.
The two persons were her and me.
Us girls had a jolly time.
It is them, surely.
Who will catch this? Me.
Them that despise me shall be lightly esteemed.
Who is there? Me.

It was not us, it was him.
Who did you see?
Who did you ask for?

Remember that pronouns must agree with their antecedents in number, gender, and person.

Correct the following errors: —

Every boy must read their own sentences.
I gave the horse oats, but he would not eat it.
Every one must read it for themselves.
I took up the little boy, and set it on my knee.

Remember that the relative *who* represents persons; *which*, animals and things; *that*, persons, animals, and things; and *what*, things.

Correct the following errors: —

I have a dog who runs to meet me.
The boy which I met was quite lame.
Those which live in glass houses must not throw stones.

REVIEW QUESTIONS.

To the Teacher. — For "Schemes," see p. 268.

How many modifications have nouns and pronouns? Name and define each. How many persons are there? Define each. How many cases are there? Define each. How do you determine the case of an explanatory noun or pronoun? What is declension? How are the forms *mine*, *yours*, etc., now used? What is the rule for forming the possessive case? What words are used only in the nominative case? What words are used only in the objective case?[1] How do you determine the number, gender, and person of pronouns?

---

[1] *Her* is used in the possessive case also.

LESSON 86.

NOUNS AND PRONOUNS — PARSING.

To the Teacher. — For general " Scheme " for parsing, see p. 271.

Select and parse all the nouns and pronouns in Lesson 53.

Model for Written Parsing. — *Elizabeth's favorite, Raleigh, was beheaded by James I.*

CLASSIFICATION.		MODIFICATIONS.				SYNTAX.
Nouns.	*Kind.*	*Person.*	*Number.*	*Gender.*	*Case.*	
Elizabeth's	Prop.	3rd.	Sing.	Fem.	Pos.	Pos. Mod. of *favorite.*
favorite	Com.	"	"	Mas.	Nom.	Sub. of *was beheaded.*
Raleigh	Prop.	"	"	"	"	Exp. Mod. of *favorite.*
James I.	"	"	"	"	Obj.	Prin. word after *by.*

To the Teacher. — Select other exercises, and continue this work as long as it may be profitable. See Lessons 56, 57, 61, 64, and 65.

LESSON 87.

COMPARISON OF ADJECTIVES.

Adjectives have one modification; viz., **Comparison**.

DEFINITIONS.

Comparison is a modification of the adjective to express the relative degree of the quality in the things compared.

The **Positive Degree** express the simple quality.

The **Comparative Degree** expresses a greater or a less degree of the quality.

Comparison of Adjectives.

The **Superlative Degree** expresses the greatest or the least degree of the quality.

RULE.— Adjectives are regularly compared by adding **er** to the positive to form the comparative, and **est** to the positive to form the superlative.

Adjectives of one syllable are generally compared regularly; adjectives of two or more syllables are often compared by prefixing *more* and *most*. To express diminution, we prefix *less* and *least*.

When there are two correct forms, choose the one that can be more easily pronounced.

Compare the following adjectives. For the spelling consult your dictionaries : —

Positive.	Comparative.	Superlative.
Lovely,	lovelier,	loveliest; *or*
lovely,	more lovely,	most lovely.

Tame, warm, beautiful, brilliant, amiable, high, mad, greedy, pretty, hot.

Some adjectives are compared irregularly. Learn the following forms : —

Positive.	Comparative.	Superlative.
Good,	better,	best.
Bad, Evil, Ill,	worse,	worst.
Little,	less,	least.
Much, Many,	more,	most.

LESSON 88.

COMPARISON OF ADJECTIVES AND ADVERBS.

Remember that, when two things or groups of things are compared, the comparative degree is commonly used; when more than two, the superlative is employed.

Caution. — Adjectives should not be doubly compared.

Correct the following errors: —

Of all the boys, George is the more industrious.
Peter was older than the twelve apostles.
Which is the longer of the rivers of America?
This was the most unkindest cut of all.
He chose a more humbler part.
My hat is more handsomer than yours.
The younger of those three boys is the smarter.
Which is the more northerly, Maine, Oregon, or Minnesota?

Caution. — Do not use adjectives and adverbs extravagantly.

Correct the following errors: —

The weather is horrid.
That dress is perfectly awful.
Your coat sits frightfully.
We had an awfully good time.
This is a tremendously hard lesson.
Harry is a mighty nice boy.

Remember that adjectives whose meaning does not admit of different degrees cannot be compared; as, *every*, *infinite*.

Comparison of Adjectives and Adverbs. 195

Use in the three different degrees such of the following adjectives as admit of comparison : —

All, serene, excellent, immortal, first, two, total, universal, three-legged, bright.

Adverbs are compared in the same manner as adjectives. The following are compared regularly. Compare them : —

Fast, often, soon, late, early.

In the preceding and in the following list, find words that may be used as adjectives.

The following are compared irregularly ; learn them : —

Positive.	Comparative.	Superlative.
Badly, Ill,	worse,	worst.
Well,	better,	best.
Little,	less,	least.
Much,	more,	most.
Far,	farther,	farthest.

Adverbs ending in **ly** are generally compared by prefixing *more* and *most*. Compare the following : —

Firmly, gracefully, actively, easily.

To the Teacher. — Let the pupils select and parse all the adjectives and adverbs in Lesson 27. Select other exercises, and continue the work as long as it is profitable. See "Schemes" for review, p. 270.

REVIEW QUESTIONS.

How is a noun parsed? What modifications have adjectives? What is comparison? How many degrees of comparison are there?

Define each. How are adjectives regularly compared? Distinguish the uses of the comparative and the superlative degree. Give the directions for using adjectives and adverbs (Lesson 88). Illustrate. What adjectives cannot be compared? How are adverbs compared?

LESSON 89.

MODIFICATION OF VERBS.

VOICE.

Hints for Oral Instruction. — "*I picked* the rose." The same thing may be said in another way. "The *rose was picked* by me." The first verb, *picked*, shows that the subject represents the actor, and the second form of the verb, *was picked*, shows that the subject names the thing acted upon. This change in the form and use of the verb is called **Voice.** The first form is called the **Active Voice**; and the second, the **Passive Voice.**

The passive form is very convenient when we wish to assert an action without naming any actor. "Money *is coined*" is better than "*Somebody coins* money."

DEFINITIONS.

Voice is that modification of the transitive verb which shows whether the subject names the **actor** or the **thing acted upon.**

The **Active Voice** shows that the subject names the actor.

The **Passive Voice** shows that the subject names the thing acted upon.

Mode, Tense, Number, and Person.

In each of the following sentences, change the voice of the verb without changing the meaning of the sentence, and note the other changes that occur in the sentence : —

The industrious bees gather honey from the flowers.
The storm drove the vessel against the rock.
Our words should be carefully chosen.
Death separates the dearest friends.
His vices have weakened his mind and destroyed his health.
True valor protects the feeble and humbles the oppressor.
The Duke of Wellington, who commanded the English armies in the Peninsula, never lost a battle.
Moses led the Israelites out of Egypt.
Dr. Livingstone explored a large part of Africa.
The English were conquered by the Normans.

Name all the transitive verbs in Lessons 20 and 22, and give their voice.

LESSON 90.
MODE, TENSE, NUMBER, AND PERSON.

Hints for Oral Instruction. — When I say, "James *walks*," I assert the walking as a fact. When I say, "James *may walk*," I do not assert the action as a fact, but as a possible action. When I say, "If James *walk* out, he will improve," I assert the action, not as an actual fact, but as a condition of James's improving — a condition that may or may not become a fact. When I say to James, "*Walk* out," I do not assert that James actually does the act, I assert the action as a command.

The action expressed by the verb *walk* is here asserted in four different ways, or **Modes**.[1] The first way is called the **Indicative Mode**; the second, the **Potential Mode**; the third, the **Subjunctive Mode**; the fourth, the **Imperative Mode**.

Let the teacher give other examples and require the pupils to repeat this instruction.

For the two forms of the verb called the **Infinitive** and the **Participle**, see "Hints," Lessons 48 and 49.

"I *walk;*" "I *walked;*" "I *shall walk.*" In each of these sentences, the manner of asserting the action is the same. "I *walk*" expresses the action as present; "I *walked*" expresses the action as past; "I *shall walk*" expresses the action as future. As **Tense** means time, the first form is called the **Present Tense**; the second, the **Past Tense**; and the third, the **Future Tense**.

We have three other forms of the verb, expressing the action as completed in the present, the past, or the future.

"I *have walked* out to-day;" "I *had walked* out when he called;" "I *shall have walked* out by to-morrow." The form, *have walked*, expressing the action as completed in the present, is called the **Present Perfect Tense**. The form, *had walked*, expressing the action as completed in the past, is called the **Past Perfect Tense**. The form,

---

[1] Many grammarians reject the potential mode, insisting that, when we assert the power, liberty, or possibility of acting or being, we assert it (1) as a fact, and the verb is in the indicative; or we assert it (2) as a supposition or conception merely, and the verb is in the subjunctive.

shall have walked, expressing an action to be completed in the future, is called the **Future Perfect Tense.**

Let the teacher give other verbs, and require the pupils to name and explain the different tenses.

"*I walk;*" "*Thou walkest;*" "*He walks;*" "*They walk.*" In the second sentence, the verb *walk* was changed by adding **est**; and in the third, it was changed by adding **s**. These changes are for the sake of agreement with the person of the subject. The verb ending in **est** agrees with the subject *thou* in the second person, and the verb ending in **s** agrees with *he* in the third person. In the fourth sentence, the subject is in the third person; but it is plural, and so the verb drops the **s** to agree with the plural *they*.

Verbs are said to agree in **Person** and **Number** with their subjects. The person and number forms may be found in Lessons 93, 94.

Definitions.

Mode is that modification of the verb which denotes the manner of asserting the action or being.

The **Indicative Mode** asserts the action or being as a fact.

The **Potential Mode** asserts the power, liberty, possibility, or necessity of acting or being.

The **Subjunctive Mode** asserts the action or being as a mere condition, supposition, or wish.

The **Imperative Mode** asserts the action or being as a command or an entreaty.

The **Infinitive** is a form of the verb which names the action or being in a general way, without asserting it of anything.

The **Participle** is a form of the verb partaking of the nature of an adjective or of a noun,[1] and expressing the action or being as assumed.

The **Present Participle** denotes action or being as continuing at the time indicated by the predicate.

The **Past Participle** denotes action or being as past or completed at the time indicated by the predicate.

The **Past Perfect Participle** denotes action or being as completed at a time previous to that indicated by the predicate.

Tense is that modification of the verb which expresses the time of the action or being.

The **Present Tense** expresses action or being as present.

The **Past Tense** expresses action or being as past.

The **Future Tense** expresses action or being as yet to come.

The **Present Perfect Tense** expresses action or being as completed at the present time.

The **Past Perfect Tense** expresses action or being as completed at some past time.

The **Future Perfect Tense** expresses action or being to be completed at some future time.

Number and **Person** of a verb are those modifications that show its agreement with the number and person of its subject.

---
[1] See Lesson 98, foot-note.

LESSON 91.

CONJUGATION OF THE VERB.

DEFINITIONS.

Conjugation is the regular arrangement of all the forms of the verb.

Synopsis is the regular arrangement of the forms of one number and person in all the modes and tenses.

Auxiliary Verbs are those that help in the conjugation of other verbs.

The auxiliaries are *do, be, have, shall, will, may, can,* and *must.*

The **Principal Parts** of a verb are the present indicative or the present infinitive, the past indicative, and the past participle.

These are called principal parts, because all the other forms of the verb are derived from them.

We give, below, the principal parts of some of the most important irregular verbs.[1] Learn them.

Present.	Past.	Past Par.
Be *or* am,	was,	been.
Begin,	began,	begun.
Blow,	blew,	blown.
Break,	broke,	broken.
Choose,	chose,	chosen.
Come,	came,	come.
Do,	did,	done.
Draw,	drew,	drawn.

[1] Most of those in the list are irregular strong verbs. See Lesson 74, foot-note.

Present.	Past.	Past Par.
Drink,	drank,	drunk.
Drive,	drove,	driven.
Eat,	ate,	eaten.
Fall,	fell,	fallen.
Fly,	flew,	flown.
Freeze,	froze,	frozen.
Go,	went,	gone.
Get,	got,	got *or* gotten.
Give,	gave,	given.
Grow,	grew,	grown.
Know,	knew,	known.
Lay,	laid,	laid.
Lie (to rest),	lay,	lain.
Ride,	rode,	ridden.
Ring,	rang *or* rung,	rung.
Rise,	rose,	risen.
Run,	ran,	run.
See,	saw,	seen.
Set,	set,	set.
Sit,	sat,	sat.
Shake,	shook,	shaken.
Sing,	sang *or* sung,	sung.
Slay,	slew,	slain.
Speak,	spoke,	spoken.
Steal,	stole,	stolen.
Swim,	swam *or* swum,	swum.
Take,	took,	taken.
Tear,	tore,	torn.
Throw,	threw,	thrown.
Wear,	wore,	worn.
Write,	wrote,	written.

Conjugation of the Verb SEE.

The following irregular verbs are called **Defective** because some of their parts are wanting:—

Present.	Past.	Present.	Past.
Can,	could.	Will,	would.
May,	might.	Must,	——
Shall,	should.	Ought,	——

LESSON 92.
CONJUGATION OF THE VERB SEE IN THE SIMPLE FORM.

PRINCIPAL PARTS.

Present.	Past.	Past Par.
See,	saw,	seen.

Indicative Mode.
PRESENT TENSE.

Singular.   *Plural.*
1. I see,   1. We see,
2. { You see, *or* Thou seest,   2. You see,
3. He sees;   3. They see.

PAST TENSE.
1. I saw,   1. We saw,
2. { You saw, *or* Thou sawest,   2. You saw,
3. He saw;   3. They saw.

FUTURE TENSE.
1. I shall see,   1. We shall see,
2. { You will see, *or* Thou wilt see,   2. You will see,
3. He will see;   3. They will see.

Present Perfect Tense.

Singular.
1. I have seen,
2. { You have seen, *or*
     Thou hast seen,
3. He has seen;

Plural.
1. We have seen,
2. You have seen,
3. They have seen.

Past Perfect Tense.

1. I had seen,
2. { You had seen, *or*
     Thou hadst seen,
3. He had seen;

1. We had seen,
2. You had seen,
3. They had seen.

Future Perfect Tense.

1. I shall have seen,
2. { You will have seen, *or*
     Thou wilt have seen,
3. He will have seen;

1. We shall have seen,
2. You will have seen,
3. They will have seen.

Potential Mode.[1]

Present Tense.

Singular.
1. I may see,
2. { You may see, *or*
     Thou mayst see,
3. He may see;

Plural.
1. We may see,
2. You may see,
3. They may see.

Past Tense.

1. I might see,
2. { You might see, *or*
     Thou mightst see,
3. He might see;

1. We might see,
2. You might see,
3. They might see.

---

[1] See Lesson 90, foot-note.

Conjugation of the Verb SEE.

PRESENT PERFECT TENSE.

Singular.   *Plural.*
1. I may have seen,   1. We may have seen,
2. { You may have seen, *or*   2. You may have seen,
    Thou mayst have seen,
3. He may have seen;   3. They may have seen.

PAST PERFECT TENSE.

1. I might have seen,   1. We might have seen,
2. { You might have seen, *or*   2. You might have seen,
    Thou mightst have seen,
3. He might have seen;   3. They might have seen.

Subjunctive Mode.
PRESENT TENSE.

Singular.   *Plural.*
1. If I see,   1. If we see,
2. { If you see, *or*   2. If you see,
    If thou see,
3. If he see;   3. If they see.

Imperative Mode.
PRESENT TENSE.

2. See (you *or* thou);   2. See (you).

Infinitives.
PRESENT TENSE.
To see.

PRESENT PERFECT TENSE.
To have seen.

Participles.

PRESENT.   PAST.   PAST PERFECT.
Seeing.   Seen.   Having seen.

To the Teacher.—Let the pupils prefix *do* and *did* to the simple present *see*, and thus make the Emphatic form of the present and the past tense.

Let *can* and *must* be used in place of *may;* and *could, would,* and *should,* in place of *might.*

Require the pupils to tell how each tense is formed, and to note all changes for agreement in number and person.

A majority of modern writers use the indicative forms instead of the subjunctive in all of the tenses, unless it may be the present. The subjunctive forms of the verb *be* are retained in the present and the past tense.

Let the pupils understand that the mode and tense forms do not always correspond with the actual meaning. "The ship *sails* next week." "I *may go* to-morrow." The verbs *sails* and *may go* are present in form but future in meaning. "If it *rains* by noon, he may not come." The verb *rains* is indicative in form but subjunctive in meaning.

The plural forms, *You saw, You were,* etc., are used in the singular also.

LESSON 93.

CONJUGATION OF THE VERB.—SIMPLE FORM.

Fill out the following forms, using the principal parts of the verb *walk*. *Pres., walk; Past, walked; Past Par., walked.*

Indicative Mode.

PRESENT TENSE.

Singular.	*Plural.*
1. I ___Pres.___ ,	1. We ___Pres.___ ,
2. { You ___Pres.___ , Thou ___Pres.___ *est,*	2. You ___Pres.___ ,
3. He ___Pres.___ *s;*	3. They ___Pres.___ .

Conjugation of the Verb.—Simple Form.

Past Tense.
Singular. *Plural.*
1. I _Past_ , 1. We _Past_ ,
2. { You _Past_ , 2. You _Past_ ,
   { Thou _Past_ **st,**
3. He _Past_ ; 3. They _Past_ .

Future Tense.
1. I *shall* _Pres._ , 1. We *shall* _Pres._ ,
2. { You *will* _Pres._ , 2. You *will* _Pres._ ,
   { Thou *wil-t* _Pres._ ,
3. He *will* _Pres._ ; 3. They *will* _Pres._ .

Present Perfect Tense.
1. I *have* _Past Par._, 1. We *have* _Past Par._,
2. { You *have* _Past Par._, 2. You *have* _Past Par._,
   { Thou *ha-st* _Past Par._,
3. He *ha-s* _Past Par._ ; 3. They *have* _Past Par._.

Past Perfect Tense.
1. I *had* _Past Par._, 1. We *had* _Past Par._,
2. { You *had* _Past Par._, 2. You *had* _Past Par._,
   { Thou *had-st* _Past Par._,
3. He *had* _Past Par._ ; 3. They *had* _Past Par._.

Future Perfect Tense.
1. I *shall have* _Past Par._, 1. We *shall have* _Past Par._,
2. { You *will have* _Past Par._, 2. You *will have* _Past Par._,
   { Thou *wil-t have* _Past Par._,
3. He *will have* _Past Par._ ; 3. They *will have* _Past Par._.

Potential Mode.

Present Tense.

Singular.		Plural.	
1. I may	_Pres._ ,	1. We may	_Pres._ ,
2. { You may	_Pres._ ,	2. You may	_Pres._ ,
Thou may-st	_Pres._ ,		
3. He may	_Pres._ ;	3. They may	_Pres._ .

Past Tense.

1. I might	_Pres._ ,	1. We might	_Pres._ ,
2. { You might	_Pres._ ,	2. You might	_Pres._ ,
Thou might-st	_Pres._ ,		
3. He might	_Pres._ ;	3. They might	_Pres._ .

Present Perfect Tense.

1. I may have	_Past Par._,	1. We may have	_Past Par._,
2. { You may have	_Past Par._,	2. You may have	_Past Par._,
Thou may-st have	_Past Par._,		
3. He may have	_Past Par._ ;	3. They may have	_Past Par._.

Past Perfect Tense.

1. I might have	_Past Par._,	1. We might have	_Past Par._,
2. { You might have	_Past Par._,	2. You might have	_Past Par._,
Thou might-st have	_Past Par._,		
3. He might have	_Past Par._ ;	3. They might have	_Past Par._.

Subjunctive Mode.

Present Tense.

Singular.		Plural.	
1. If I	_Pres._ ,	1. If we	_Pres._ ,
2. { If you	_Pres._ ,	2. If you	_Pres._ ,
If thou	_Pres._ ,		
3. If he	_Pres._ ;	3. If they	_Pres._ .

Conjugation of the Verb BE.

Imperative Mode.
PRESENT TENSE.
Singular.   *Plural.*
2. *Pres.* (you *or* thou) ;   2. *Pres.* (you).

Infinitives.
PRESENT TENSE.
To *Pres.* .

PRESENT PERFECT TENSE.
To have *Past Par.*.

Participles.
PRESENT.   PAST.   PAST PERFECT.
Pres. ing.   *Past Par.*   Having *Past Par.*

To the Teacher. — Let the pupils fill out these forms with other verbs. In the indicative, present, third, singular, es is sometimes added instead of s ; and in the second person, old style, st is sometimes added instead of est.

LESSON 94.
CONJUGATION OF THE VERB BE.

In studying this Lesson, pay no attention to the line at the right of each verb.

Indicative Mode.
PRESENT TENSE.
Singular.   *Plural.*
1. I am ——,   1. We are ——,
2. { You are ——, *or*   2. You are ——,
     Thou art ——,
3. He is —— ;   3. They are ——.

Past Tense.

Singular.

1. I was ——.
2. { You were ——, *or*
   { Thou wast ——,
3. He was —— ;

Plural.

1. We were ——,
2. You were ——,
3. They were ——.

Future Tense.

1. I shall be ——,
2. { You will be ——, *or*
   { Thou wilt be ——,
3. He will be —— ;

1. We shall be ——,
2. You will be ——,
3. They will be ——.

Present Perfect Tense.

1. I have been ——,
2. { You have been ——, *or*
   { Thou hast been ——,
3. He has been —— ;

1. We have been ——,
2. You have been ——,
3. They have been ——.

Past Perfect Tense.

1. I had been ——,
2. { You had been ——, *or*
   { Thou hadst been ——,
3. He had been —— ;

1. We had been ——,
2. You had been ——,
3. They had been ——.

Future Perfect Tense.

1. I shall have been ——,
2. { You will have been ——, *or*
   { Thou wilt have been ——,
3. He will have been —— ;

1. We shall have been ——,
2. You will have been ——,
3. They will have been ——.

Potential Mode.

Present Tense.
Singular. *Plural.*

1. I may be ———,   1. We may be ———,
2. { You may be ———, *or*   2. You may be ———,
   { Thou mayst be ———,
3. He may be ———;   3. They may be ———.

Past Tense.

1. I might be ———,   1. We might be ———,
2. { You might be ———, *or*   2. You might be ———,
   { Thou mightst be ———,
3. He might be ———,   3. They might be ———·

Present Perfect Tense.

1. I may have been ———,   1. We may have been ———,
2. { You may have been ———, *or*   2. You may have been ———,
   { Thou mayst have been ———,
3. He may have been ———;   3. They may have been ———.

Past Perfect Tense.

1. I might have been ———,   1. We might have been ———,
2. { You might have been ———, *or*   2. You might have been ———,
   { Thou mightst have been ———,
3. He might have been ———;   3. They might have been ———.

Subjunctive Mode.

Present Tense.
Singular. *Plural.*

1. If I be ———,   1. If we be ———,
2. { If you be ———, *or*   2. If you be ———,
   { If thou be ———,
3. If he be ———;   3. If they be ———.

PAST TENSE.
Singular.   *Plural.*
1. If I were ——,   1. If we were ——,
2. { If you were ——, *or*
    If thou wert ——,   2. If you were ——,
3. If he were ——;   3. If they were ——.

Imperative Mode.
PRESENT TENSE.
2. Be (you *or* thou) ——;   2. Be (you) ——.

Infinitives.
PRESENT TENSE.
To be ——.

PRESENT PERFECT TENSE.
To have been ——.

Participles.
PRESENT.   PAST.   PAST PERFECT.
Being ——.   Been.   Having been ——.

To the Teacher. — After the pupils have become thoroughly familiar with the verb *be* as a principal verb, teach them to use it as an auxiliary in making the **Progressive Form** and the **Passive Form.**

The progressive form may be made by filling all the blanks with the present participle of some verb.

The passive form may be made by filling all the blanks with the past participle of a transitive verb.

Notice that there is no blank after the past participle.

In the progressive form, this participle is wanting; and in the passive form, it is the same as in the simple.

LESSON 95.

AGREEMENT OF THE VERB.

Remember that the verb must agree with its subject in number and person.

Give the person and number of each of the following verbs, and write sentences in which each form shall be used correctly : —

Common forms. — Does, has = ha(ve)s, is, am, are, was, were.

Old forms. — Seest, sawest, hast = ha(ve)st, wilt, mayst, mightst, art, wast.

When a verb has two or more subjects connected by *and*, it must agree with them in the plural. A similar rule applies to the agreement of the pronoun.

Correct the following errors : —

Poverty and obscurity *oppresses* him who thinks that *it is* oppressive.

Wrong ; the verb *oppresses* should be *oppress* to agree with its two subjects connected by *and*. The pronoun *it* should be *they* to agree with its two antecedents, and the verb *is* should be *are* to agree with *they*.

Industry, energy, and good sense is essential to success.
Time and tide waits for no man.
The tall sunflower and the little violet is turning its face to the sun.
The mule and the horse was harnessed together.
Every green leaf and every blade of grass seem grateful.

Wrong; the verb *seem* should be singular; for, when several singular subjects are preceded by *each*, *every*, or *no*, they are taken separately.

Correct the following errors: —

Each day and each hour bring their portion of duty.
Every book and every paper were found in their place.

When a verb has two or more singular subjects connected by *or* or *nor*, it must agree with them in the singular. A similar rule applies to the agreement of the pronoun.

Correct the following errors: —

One or the other have made a mistake in their statement.
Neither the aster nor the dahlia are cultivated for their fragrance.
Either the president or his secretary were responsible.
Neither Ann, Jane, nor Sarah are at home.

To foretell, or to express future time simply, the auxiliary *shall* is used in the first person, and *will* in the second and third; but, when a speaker determines or promises, he uses *will* in the first person and *shall* in the second and third.

Correct the following errors: —

I will freeze if I do not move about.
You shall feel better soon, I think.
She shall be fifteen years old to-morrow.
I shall find it for you if you shall bring the book to me.
You will have it if I can get it for you.

He will have it if he shall take the trouble to ask for it.
He will not do it if I can prevent him.
I will drown, nobody shall help me.
I will be obliged to you if you shall attend to it.
We will have gone by to-morrow morning.
You shall disappoint your father if you do not return.
I do not think I will like the change.
Next Tuesday shall be your birthday.
You shall be late if you do not hurry.

LESSON 96.
ERRORS IN THE FORM OF THE VERB.

When the past tense and the past participle differ in form, they are often confounded in use; as, "I *done* it;" "I *seen* it."

If the pupils are required to construct short sentences, using the Past forms in Lesson 91 as predicates, and the Past Participle forms as modifiers or as completing words in compound verbs, they may reach some such conclusions as these : —

The Past is always an asserting, or predicate, word; the Past Participle never asserts, but is used as an adjective modifier or as the completing word of a compound verb; the Present may be used as a predicate or as an infinitive.

Copy, and repeat aloud, these exercises : —

1. *Lay* down your pen.
2. *Lie* down, Rover.
3. I *laid* down my pen.
4. The dog then *lay* down.

5. I have *laid* down my pen.
6. The dog has *lain* down.
7. *Set* the pail down.
8. *Sit* down and rest.
9. I then *set* it down.
10. I *sat* down and rested.
11. I have *set* it down.
12. I have *sat* down.
13. My work was *laid* aside.
14. I was *lying* down.
15. The trap was *set* by the river.
16. I was *sitting* by the river.
17. The garment *sits* well.
18. The hen *sits* on her eggs.
19. He came in and *lay* down.
20. The Mediterranean *lies* between Europe and Africa.

We may speak of *laying* something or *setting* something, or may say that something is *laid* or is *set;* but we cannot speak of *lying* or *sitting* something, or of something being *lain* or *sat*. *Set*, in some of its meanings, is used without an object; as, "The sun *set;*" "He *set* out on a journey." *Set* is generally transitive; *sit*, always intransitive. *Lay* is transitive; *lie*, intransitive.

Lay, the present of the first verb, and *lay*, the past of *lie*, may easily be distinguished by the difference in meaning and in the time expressed.

Correct the following errors : —

Those things *have* not *came* to-day.

Wrong; because the past *came* is here used for the past participle *come*. The present perfect tense is formed by prefixing *have* to the past participle.

I done all my work before breakfast.
I come in a little late yesterday.
He has went to my desk without permission.

Errors in the Form of the Verb.

That stupid fellow set down on my new hat.
He sat the chair in the corner.
Sit that plate on the table and let it set.
I have set in this position a long time.
That child will not lay still or set still a minute.
I laid down under the tree and enjoyed the scenery.
Lie that stick on the table and let it lay.
Those boys were drove out of the fort three times.
I have rode through the park.
I done what I could.
He has not spoke to-day.
The leaves have fell from the trees.
This sentence is wrote badly.
He throwed his pen down and said that the point was broke.
He teached me grammar.
I seen him when he done it.
My hat was took off my head and throwed out of the window.
The bird has flew into that tall tree.
I was chose leader.
I have began to do better. I begun this morning.
My breakfast was ate in a hurry.
Your dress sets well.
That foolish old hen is setting on a wooden egg.
He has tore it up and throwed it away.
William has took my knife, and I am afraid he has stole it.
This should be well shook.
I begun to sing before I knowed what I was doing.
We drunk from a pure spring.
I thought you had forsook us.
His pencil is nearly wore up.
He come and tell me all he knowed about it.

LESSON 97.

REVIEW QUESTIONS.

To the Teacher. — See "Scheme," p. 269.

How many modifications have verbs? *Ans.* — Five; viz., voice, mode, tense, number, and person. Define voice. How many voices are there? What verbs have voice? Define each. Illustrate. What is mode? How many modes are there? What mode is rejected by some? Define each. What is an infinitive? What is a participle? How many different kinds of participles are there? Define each. Illustrate. What is tense? How many tenses are there? Define each. Illustrate. What are the number and the person of a verb? Illustrate. What is conjugation? What is synopsis? What are auxiliaries? Name the auxiliaries. What are the principal parts of a verb? Why are they so called? How does a verb agree with its subject? When a verb has two or more subjects, how does it agree? Illustrate the uses of *shall* and *will*. Of *lie, lay, sit,* and *set*.

To the Teacher. — Select some of the preceding exercises, and require the pupils to write the parsing of all the verbs. See Lessons 34, 35, 48, 49, and 56.

Model for Written Parsing — Verbs. — *The Yankee, selling his farm, wanders away to seek new lands.*

CLASSIFICATION.		MODIFICATIONS.					SYNTAX.
Verbs.	*Kind.*	*Voice.*	*Mode.*	*Tense.*	*Num.*	*Per.*	
[1] selling	Pr. Par., Ir., Tr.	Ac.	—	—	—	—	Mod. of *Yankee.*
wanders	Reg., Int.	—	Ind.	Pres.	Sing.	3d.	Pred. of "
[1] seek	Inf., Ir., Tr.	Ac.	—	"	—	—	Prin. word in phrase Mod. of *wanders.*

[1] Participles and Infinitives have no person or number.

LESSON 98.

COMPOSITION.

Participles[1] sometimes partake of the nature of the noun while they retain the nature of the verb.

Use each of these phrases in a sentence, and explain the nature of the word in **ing** : —

Model. — " —— *in building* a snow *fort;* " " They were engaged *in building* a snow *fort.*" *Building*, like a noun, follows the preposition *in*, as the principal word in the phrase; and, like a verb, it takes the object complement *fort*.

—— by foretelling storms. —— by helping others. —— on approaching the house. —— in catching fish.

Use the following phrases as subjects : —

Walking in the garden ——. His writing that letter ——. Breaking a promise ——.

Use each of these phrases in a complex sentence, letting some of the dependent clauses modify as adjectives, and some as adverbs : —

—— in sledges. —— up the Hudson. —— down the Rhine. —— through the Alps. —— with snow and ice. —— into New York Bay. —— on the prairie. —— at Saratoga.

Build a short sentence containing all the parts of speech.

---

[1] If different names for the words in ing that have an adjective use and for those that have a noun use are desired, retain **participle** for the first and assign **nounal verb** to the second. We suggest these distinguishing names in "Higher Lessons," and use them in the "High School Grammar."

Expand the following simple sentence into twelve sentences: —

Astronomy teaches the size, form, nature, and motions of the sun, moon, and stars.

Contract the following awkward compound sentence into a neat simple sentence: —

Hannibal passed through Gaul, and then he crossed the Alps, and then came down into Italy, and then he defeated several Roman generals.

Change the following complex sentences to compound sentences: —

When he asked me the question, I answered him courteously.

Morse, the man who invented the telegraph, was a public benefactor.

When spring comes, the birds will return.

Contract the following complex sentences into simple sentences by changing the verb in the dependent clause to the form in **ing**: —

A ship which was gliding along the horizon attracted our attention.

I saw a man who was plowing a field.

When the shower had passed, we went on our way.

I heard that he wrote that article.

That he was a foreigner was well known.

I am not sure that he did it.

Every pupil who has an interest in this work will prepare for it.

Change the following compound sentences to complex sentences : —

Model. — Morning dawns, and the clouds disperse =
When morning dawns, the clouds disperse.

Avoid swearing ; it is a wicked habit.
Pearls are valuable, and they are found in oyster shells.
Dickens wrote David Copperfield, and he died in 1870.
Some animals are vertebrates, and they have a backbone.

Expand each of the following sentences as much as you properly may : —

Indians dance. The clock struck. The world moves.

LESSON 99.

MISCELLANEOUS ERRORS.

Correct the following errors : —

I have got that book at home.

Wrong; because *have*, alone, asserts possession. *Got*, used in the sense of *obtained*, is correct; as, "I have just *got the book*."

Have you got time to help me?
There is many mistakes in my composition.

Wrong; because *is* should agree with its plural subject *mistakes*. The adverb *there* is often used to introduce a sentence, that the subject may follow the predicate. This often makes the sentence smooth and gives variety.

There goes my mother and sister.
Here comes the soldiers.
There was many friends to greet him.
It ain't there.

Ain't is a vulgar contraction. Correction — It *is not* there.

I have made up my mind that it ain't no use.
'Tain't so bad as you think.
Two years' interest were due.
Every one of his acts were criticised.
I, Henry, and you have been chosen.

Wrong; for politeness requires that you should mention the one spoken to, first; the one spoken of, next; and yourself, last.

He invited you and I and Mary.
Me and Jane are going to the fair.
I only want a little piece.
He is a handsome, tall man.
Did you sleep good?
How much trouble one has, don't they?
He inquired for some tinted ladies' note paper.
You needn't ask me nothing about it,
  for I haven't got no time to answer.
Him that is diligent will succeed.
He found the place sooner than me.
Who was that? It was me and him.
If I was her, I would say less.
Bring me them tongs.
Us boys have a baseball club.
Whom did you say that it was?

Who did you speak to just now?
Who did you mean when you said that?
Where was you when I called?
There's twenty of us going.
Circumstances alters cases.
Tell them to set still.
He laid down by the fire.
She has lain her book aside.
It takes him everlastingly.
That was an elegant old rock.

LESSON 100.

ANALYSIS AND PARSING.

1. Thou shalt not take the name of the Lord thy God in vain.
2. Strike! till the last armed foe expires!
3. You wrong me, Brutus.
4. Shall we gather strength by irresolution and inaction?
5. Why stand we here idle?
6. Give me liberty or give me death!
7. Thy mercy, O Lord, is in the heavens, and thy faithfulness reacheth unto the clouds.
8. The clouds poured out water, the skies sent out a sound, the voice of thy thunder was in the heaven.
9. The heavens declare his righteousness, and all the people see his glory.
10. The verdant lawn, the shady grove, the variegated landscape, the boundless ocean, and the starry firmament are beautiful and magnificent objects.
11. When you grind your corn, give not the flour to the devil and the bran to God.

12. That which the fool does in the end the wise man does at the beginning.
13. Xerxes commanded the largest army that was ever brought into the field.
14. Without oxygen, fires would cease to burn, and all animals would immediately die.
15. Liquids, when acted upon by gravity, press downward, upward, and sideways.
16. Matter exists in three states — the solid state, the liquid state, and the gaseous state.
17. The blending of the seven prismatic colors produces white light.
18. Soap-bubbles, when they are exposed to light, exhibit colored rings.
19. He who yields to temptation debases himself with a debasement from which he can never arise.

20. Young eyes that last year smiled in ours
    Now point the rifle's barrel;
    And hands then stained with fruits and flowers
    Bear redder stains of quarrel.

CAPITAL LETTERS AND PUNCTUATION.

Capital Letters. — The first word of (1) a sentence, (2) a line of poetry, (3) a direct quotation making complete sense and a direct question introduced into a sentence. and (4) phrases or clauses separately numbered or paragraphed should begin with a capital letter. Begin with a capital letter (5) proper names and words derived from them, (6) names of things personified, and (7) most abbreviations. Write in capital letters (8) the words *I* and *O*, and (9) numbers in the Roman notation.[1]

Examples. — 1. The judicious are always a minority.
2. Honor and shame from no condition rise;
Act well your part, there all the honor lies.
3. The question is, "Can law make people honest?" 4. Paintings are useful for these reasons : 1. They please; 2. They instruct.
5. The heroic Nelson destroyed the French fleet in Aboukir Bay.
6. Next, Anger rushed, his eyes on fire. 7. The Atlantic ocean beat Mrs. Partington. 8. The use of *O* and *oh* I am now to explain.
9. Napoleon II. never came to the throne.

Period. — Place a period after (1) a declarative and an imperative sentence, (2) an abbreviation, and (3) a number written in the Roman notation.

For examples see 1, 7, and 9 above.

Interrogation Point. — Every direct interrogative sentence or clause should be followed by an interrogation point.

Example. — King Agrippa, believest thou the prophets?

Exclamation Point. — All exclamatory expressions must be followed by the exclamation point.

Example. — Oh! bloodiest picture in the book of time!

---

[1] Smaller letters are preferred where numerous references to chapters, etc., are made.

Comma. — Set off by the comma (1) a phrase out of its natural order or not closely connected with the word it modifies; (2) an explanatory modifier that does not restrict the modified term or combine closely with it; (3) a participle used as an adjective modifier, with the words belonging to it, unless restrictive; (4) the adjective clause when not restrictive; (5) the adverb clause unless it closely follows and restricts the word it modifies; (6) a word or phrase independent or nearly so; (7) a direct quotation introduced into a sentence, unless formally introduced; (8) a noun clause used as an attribute complement; and (9) a term connected to another by *or* and having the same meaning. Separate by the comma (10) connected words and phrases unless all the conjunctions are expressed; (11) independent clauses when short and closely connected; and (12) the parts of a compound predicate and of other phrases when long or differently modified.

Examples. — 1. In the distance, icebergs look like masses of burnished metal. 2. Alexandria, the capital of Lower Egypt, is an ill-looking city. 3. Labor, diving deep into the earth, brings up long-hidden stores of coal. 4. The sun, which is the center of our system, is millions of miles from us. 5. When beggars die, there are no comets seen. 6. Gentlemen, this, then, is your verdict. 7. God said, "Let there be light." 8. Nelson's signal was, "England expects every man to do his duty." 9. Rubbers, or overshoes, are worn to keep the feet dry. 10. The sable, the seal, and the otter furnish us rich furs. 11. His dark eye flashed, his proud breast heaved, his cheek's hue came and went. 12. Flights of birds darken the air, and tempt the traveler with the promise of abundant provisions.

Semicolon. — Independent clauses (1) when slightly connected, or (2) when themselves divided by the comma, must be separated by the semicolon. Use the semicolon (3) between serial phrases or clauses having a common dependence on something that precedes or follows; and (4) before *as, viz., to wit, namely, i.e.*, and *that is*, when they introduce examples or illustrations.

Examples. — 1. The furnace blazes; the anvil rings; the busy wheels whirl round. 2. As Cæsar loved me, I weep for him; as he was fortunate, I rejoice at it; as he was valiant, I honor him; but, as he was ambitious, I slew him. 3. He drew a picture of the sufferings of our Saviour; his trial before Pilate; his ascent of Calvary; his crucifixion and death. 4. Gibbon writes, "I have been sorely afflicted with gout in the hand; to wit, laziness."

Colon. — Use the colon (1) between the parts of a sentence when these parts are themselves divided by the semicolon; and (2) before a quotation or an enumeration of particulars when formally introduced.

Examples. — 1. Canning's features were handsome; his eye, though deeply ensconced under his eyebrows, was full of sparkle and gayety: the features of Brougham were harsh in the extreme. 2. To Lentulus and Gellius bear this message: "Their graves are measured."

Dash. — Use the dash where there is an omission (1) of letters or figures, and (2) of such words as *as, namely*, or *that is*, introducing illustrations or equivalent expressions. Use the dash (3) where the sentence breaks off abruptly, and the same thought is resumed after a slight suspension, or another takes its place; and (4) before a word or phrase repeated at intervals for emphasis. The dash may be used (5) instead of marks of parenthesis, and may (6) follow other marks, adding to their force.

Examples. — 1. In M——w, ver. 3-11, you may find the "beatitudes." 2. There are two things certain in this world — taxes and death. 3. I said — I know not what. 4. I never would lay down my arms — *never* — NEVER — NEVER. 5. Fulton started a steamboat — he called it the Clermont — on the Hudson in 1807. 6. My dear Sir, — I write this letter for information.

Marks of Parenthesis. — Marks of parenthesis may be used to inclose what has no essential connection with the rest of the sentence.

Example. — The noun (Lat. *nomen*, a name) is the first part of speech.

Apostrophe. — Use the apostrophe (1) to mark the omission of letters, (2) in the pluralizing of letters, figures, and characters, and (3) to distinguish the possessive from other cases.

Examples. — 1. Bo't of John Jones 10 lbs. of butter. 2. What word is there one-half of which is *p's* ? 3. He washed the disciples' feet.

Hyphen. — Use the hyphen (-) (1) between the parts of compound words that have not become consolidated, and (2) between syllables when a word is divided.

Examples. — 1. Work-baskets are convenient. 2. Divide *basket* thus: *bas-ket*.

Quotation Marks. — Use quotation marks to inclose a copied word or passage. If the quotation contains a quotation, the latter is inclosed within single marks.

Example. — The sermon closed with this sentence, "God said. 'Let there be light.'"

Brackets. — Use brackets [ ] to inclose what, in quoting another's words, you insert by way of explanation or correction.

Example. — The Psalmist says, "I prevented [anticipated] the dawning of the morning."

LETTER-WRITING.

In writing a letter there are six things to consider — the **heading**, the **introduction**, the **body of the letter**, the **conclusion**, the **folding**, and the **superscription**.

THE HEADING.

Parts. — The Heading consists of the name of the **Place** at which the letter is written, and the **Date**. If you write from a city, give the door-number, the name of the street, the name of the city, and the name of the state. If you are at a hotel or a school or any other well-known institution, its name may take the place of the door-number and the name of the street. If you write from a village or other country place, give your post-office address, the name of the county, and that of the state.

The Date consists of the name of the month, the day of the month, and the year.

How Written. — Begin the Heading about an inch and a half from the top of the page — on the first ruled line of commercial note — and a little to the left of the middle of the page. If the Heading is very short, it may stand on one line. If it occupies more than one line, the second line should begin further to the right than the first, and the third further to the right than the second.

The Date stands upon a line by itself if the heading occupies two or more lines.

The door-number, the day of month, and the year are written in figures; the rest, in words. Each important word begins with a capital letter, each item is set off by the comma, and the whole closes with a period.

Study what has been said, and write the following headings according to these models : —

1. Hull, Mass., Nov. 1, 1860.
2. 1466 Colorado Ave., Rochester, N.Y., Apr. 3, 1870.
3. Newburyport, Mass., June 30, 1900.
4. Starkville, Herkimer Co., N.Y., Dec. 19, 1871.

1. n y rondout 11 1849 oct.   2. staten island port richmond 1877 25 january.   3. brooklyn march 1871 mansion house 29.   4. executive chamber vt february montpelier 1869 27.   5. washington franklin co mo nov 16 1874.   6. fifth ave may new york 460 9 1901.   7. washington d c march 1900 520 pennsylvania ave 16.

THE INTRODUCTION.

Parts. — The Introduction consists of the **Address** — the Name, the Title, and the Place of Business or the Residence of the one addressed — and the **Salutation**. Titles of respect and courtesy should appear in the Address. Prefix *Mr.* (plural, *Messrs.*) to a man's name; *Master* to a boy's name; *Miss* to the name of a girl or an unmarried lady; *Mrs.* to the name of a married lady. Prefix *Dr.* to the name of a physician, or write *M.D.* after his name. Prefix *Rev.* (or *The Rev.*) to the name of a clergyman; if he is a Doctor of Divinity, prefix *Rev. Dr.*, or write *Rev.* before his name and *D.D.* after it; if you do not know his Christian name, prefix *Rev. Mr.* or *Rev. Dr.* to his surname, but never *Rev.* alone. *Esq.* is added to the name of a lawyer, and to the names of other prominent men. Avoid such combinations as the following: *Mr. John Smith, Esq.; Dr. John Smith, M.D.; Mr. John Smith, M.D.*

Salutations vary with the station of the one addressed, or the writer's degree of intimacy with him. Strangers may be addressed as *Sir, Rev. Sir, General, Madam, Miss Brown*, etc.; acquaintances as *Dear Sir, Dear Madam*, etc.; friends as *My dear Sir, My dear Madam, My dear Mr. Brown*, etc.; and near relatives and other dear friends as *My dear Wife, My dear Boy, Dearest Ellen*, etc.

How Written. — The Address may follow the Heading, beginning on the next line or the next but one, and standing on the left side of the page; or it may stand in corresponding position after the Body of the Letter and the Conclusion. If the letter is written to a very intimate friend, the Address may appropriately be placed at the bottom of the letter; but in other letters, especially those on ordinary business, it should be placed at the top and as directed above. There should always be a narrow margin on the left-hand side of the page, and the Address should always begin on the marginal line. If the Address occupies more than one line, the initial words of these lines should slope to the right as in the Heading.

Begin the Salutation on the marginal line or a little to the right of it, when the Address occupies three lines; on the marginal line or further to the right than the second line of the Address begins, when this occupies two lines; a little to the right of the marginal line, when the Address occupies one line; on the marginal line, when the Address stands below.

Every important word in the Address should begin with a capital letter. All the items of it should be set off by the comma; and, as it is an abbreviated sentence, it should close with a period. Every important word in the Salutation should begin with a capital letter, and the whole should be followed by a comma.

Study what has been said, and write the following introductions according to these models: —

1. Dear Father,
   I write, etc.
2. The Rev. M. H. Buckham, D.D.,
   President of U. V. M.,
   Burlington, Vt.
   My dear Sir,
3. Messrs. Clark & Brown,
   Quogue, N.Y.
   Gentlemen,
4. Messrs. Tiffany & Co.,
   2 Milk St., Boston.
   Dear Sirs,

Letter-Writing. 233

1. henry s snow lld president of polytechnic institute brooklyn n y dear sir. 2. dr john h hobart burge 64 livingston st brooklyn n y sir. 3. prof geo n boardman chicago ill dear teacher. 4. to the president executive mansion washington d c mr president. 5. rev t k bunker elmira n y sir. 6. messrs gilbert & sons gentlemen mass boston. 7. mr george r curtis minn rochester my friend dear. 8. to the honorable john hay secretary of state washington d c sir.

THE BODY OF THE LETTER.

The Beginning. — Begin the Body of the Letter at the end of the Salutation, and on the same line if the Introduction consists of four lines — in which case the comma after the Salutation should be followed by a dash; otherwise, on the line below.

Style. — Be perspicuous. Paragraph and punctuate as in other kinds of writing. Spell correctly; write legibly, neatly, and with care. A letter tells a great deal of the writer — more, oftentimes, than the writer means to say or supposes that he is saying.

Letters of friendship should be natural, familiar, and colloquial. Whatever is interesting to you will be interesting to your friends.

Business letters should be brief, and the sentences should be short, concise, and to the point.

In formal notes the third person is generally used instead of the first and second; there is no Introduction, no Conclusion, no Signature, only the name of the Place and the Date at the bottom, on the left side of the page.

THE CONCLUSION.

Parts.—The Conclusion consists of the **Complimentary Close** and the **Signature**. The forms of the Complimentary Close are many, and are determined by the relations of the writer to the one addressed. In letters of friendship, you may use *Your sincere friend; Yours affectionately; Your loving son* or *daughter*, etc. In business letters, you may use *Yours; Yours truly; Truly yours; Yours respectfully; Very respectfully yours*, etc. In official letters, use *I have the honor to be, Sir, your obedient servant; Very respectfully, your most obedient servant.*

The Signature consists of your Christian name and your surname. In addressing a stranger write your Christian name in full. A lady addressing a stranger should prefix her title—*Miss* or *Mrs.*—to her own name, enclosing it within marks of parenthesis if she wishes.

How Written.—The Conclusion should begin near the middle of the first line below the Body of the Letter, and should slope to the right like the Heading and the Address. Begin each line of it with a capital letter, and punctuate as in other writing, following the whole with a period. The Signature should be very plain.

THE FOLDING.

The Folding is a simple matter when, as now, the envelope used is adapted in length to the width of the sheet. Take the letter as it lies before you, with its first page uppermost, turn up the bottom of it about one-third the length of the sheet, bring the top down over this, taking care that the sides are even, and press the parts together. Taking the envelope with its back toward you, insert the letter, putting in first the edge last folded.

The form of the envelope may require the letter to be folded in the middle. Other conditions may require other ways of folding.

THE SUPERSCRIPTION.

Parts. — The Superscription is what is written on the outside of the envelope. It is the same as the Address, consisting of the Name, the Title, and the full Directions of the one addressed.

How Written. — The Superscription should begin near the middle of the envelope and near the left edge — the envelope lying with its closed side toward you — and should occupy three or four lines. These lines should slope to the right as in the Heading and the Address, the spaces between the lines should be the same, and the last line should end near the lower right-hand corner. On the first line the Name and the Title should stand. If the one addressed is in a city, the door-number and name of the street should be on the second line, the name of the city on the third, and the name of the state on the fourth. If he is in the country, the name of the post office should be on the second line, the name of the county on the third (or by itself near the lower left-hand corner), and the name of the state on the fourth. The titles following the name should be separated from it and from each other by the comma, and every line should end with a comma, except the last, which should be followed by a period. The lines should be straight, and every part of the Superscription should be legible. Place the stamp at the upper right-hand corner.

We give, on succeeding pages, a few letters illustrating the various forms used.

LETTER, ORDERING MERCHANDISE.

Newburgh, N.Y.,
Jan. 7, 1899.
Messrs. Hyde & Co.,
250 Broadway, N.Y.
Gentlemen,
Please send me by Adams Express the articles mentioned in the enclosed list.

Be careful in the selection of the goods, as I desire them for a special class of customers.

When they are forwarded, please inform me by letter and enclose the invoice.

Yours truly,
Thomas Dodds.

ANSWER, INCLOSING INVOICE.

250 Broadway, N.Y.,
Jan. 9, 1899.

Mr. Thomas Dodds,
Newburgh, N.Y.

Dear Sir,

We have to-day sent you by Adams Express the goods ordered in your letter of the 7th inst. Enclosed you will find the invoice. We hope that everything will reach you in good condition and will prove satisfactory in quality and in price.

Very truly yours,
Peter Hyde & Co.

INVOICE.

Thomas Dodds,
Bought of Peter Hyde & Co.

3 boxes Sperm Candles, 140 lbs.,	@ 33c.	$46 20
7 do. Adamantine Extra Candles, 182 lbs.,	" 26c.	47 32
120 lbs. Crushed Sugar,	" 12½c.	15 00
60 do. Coffee do.,	" 11¼c.	6 75
		$115 27

LETTER OF APPLICATION.

176 Clinton St., Brooklyn, N.Y.,
Dec. 12, 1899.
Messrs. Fisk & Hatch,
5 Nassau St., N.Y.
Gentlemen,
  Learning by advertisement that a clerkship in your house is vacant, I beg leave to offer myself as a candidate for the place.
 I am sixteen years old, and am strong and in excellent health. I have just graduated with honor from the seventh grade of the Polytechnic Institute, Brooklyn, and I enclose testimonials of my character and standing from the President of that Institution.
 If you desire a personal interview, I shall be glad to present myself at such time and place as you may name.
   Very respectfully yours,
    Charles Hastings.

NOTES OF INVITATION AND ACCEPTANCE

(IN THE THIRD PERSON).

Mr. and Mrs. Brooks request the pleasure of Mr. Churchill's company at a social gathering, next Tuesday evening, at 8 o'clock.

32 W. 31st Street, Oct. 5.

Mr. Churchill has much pleasure in accepting Mr. and Mrs. Brooks's kind invitation to a social gathering, next Tuesday evening.

160 Fifth Ave., Oct. 5.

LETTER OF INTRODUCTION.

Concord, N. H.,
Jan. 28, 1899.

George Chapman, Esq.,
Portland, Conn.

My dear Friend,

It gives me great pleasure to introduce to you my friend, Mr. Alpheus Crane. Any attentions you may be able to show him I shall esteem as a personal favor.

Sincerely yours,
Peter Cooper.

A Letter of Friendship.

21 Dean St., Toledo, Ohio,
Dec. 16, 1899.

My dear Mother,
 I cannot tell you how I long to be at home again and in my old place. In my dreams and in my waking hours, I am often back at the old homestead; my thoughts play truant while I pore over my books, and even while I listen to my teacher in the class-room. I would give so much to know what you all are doing — so much to feel that now and then I am in your thoughts, and that you do indeed "miss

me at home."
Everything here is as pleasant as it need be or can be, I suppose. I am sure I shall enjoy it all by and by, when I get over this fit of homesickness.
My studies are not too hard, and my teachers are kind and faithful.
Do write me a long letter as soon as you get this, and tell me everything.
Much love to each of the dear ones at home.
Your affectionate son,
Henry James.
[1] Mrs. Alexander James,
Tallmadge, Ohio.

---

[1] In familiar (and official) letters, the Address may stand, you will remember, at the bottom.

Letter-Writing.

Mrs. Alexander James,
Tallmadge,
Summit Co.   Ohio.

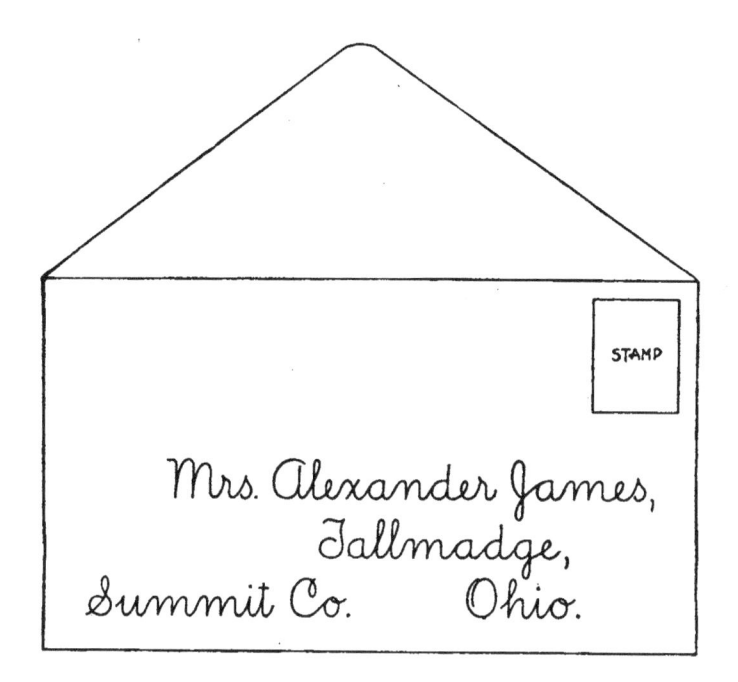

To the Teacher. — Have your pupils write complete letters and notes of all kinds. You can name the persons to whom these are to be addressed. Attend minutely to all the points. Letters of introduction should have the word *Introducing* (followed by the name of the one introduced) at the lower left-hand corner of the envelope. This letter should not be sealed. The receiver may seal it before handing it to the one addressed.

Continue this work of letter-writing until the pupils have mastered all the details, and are able easily and quickly to write any ordinary letter.

A SUMMARY OF THE RULES OF SYNTAX.

I. A noun or pronoun used as subject or as attribute complement of a predicate verb, or used independently, is in the nominative case.

II. The attribute complement of a participle or an infinitive is in the same case (nominative or objective) as the word to which it relates.

III. A noun or pronoun used as possessive modifier is in the possessive case.

IV. A noun or pronoun used as object or objective complement, or as the principal word of a prepositional phrase, is in the objective case.

V. A noun or pronoun used as explanatory modifier is in the same case as the word explained.

VI. A pronoun agrees with its antecedent in person, number, and gender.

With two or more antecedents connected by *and*, the pronoun is plural.

With two or more singular antecedents connected by *or* or *nor*, the pronoun is singular.

VII. A verb agrees with its subject in person and number.

With two or more subjects connected by *and*, the verb is plural.

With two or more singular subjects connected by *or* or *nor*, the verb is singular.

VIII. A participle assumes the action or being, and is used like an adjective or a noun.

IX. An infinitive is generally introduced by *to*, and with it forms a phrase used as a noun, an adjective, or an adverb.

X. Adjectives modify nouns or pronouns.

XI. Adverbs modify verbs, adjectives, or adverbs.

XII. A preposition introduces a phrase modifier, and shows the relation, in sense, of its principal word to the word modified.

XIII. Conjunctions connect words, phrases, or clauses.

XIV. Interjections are used independently.

Proof-Marks.

Remark.—The following are some of the marks used in correcting proof-sheets for the printer:—

- ꝺ Dē-le = Strike out.
- ∧ Cā-ret = Something to be inserted.
- | This calls attention to points or letters placed in the margin as corrections.
- ⊙ This calls attention to the period.
- *tr.* Transpose.
- ¶ Begin a new paragraph with the word preceded by [.
- *No* ¶ No new paragraph.
- V̇ This calls attention to the apostrophe.

To the Teacher.—We suggest that the pupils learn to use these marks in correcting compositions. The following exercises are given as illustrations:—

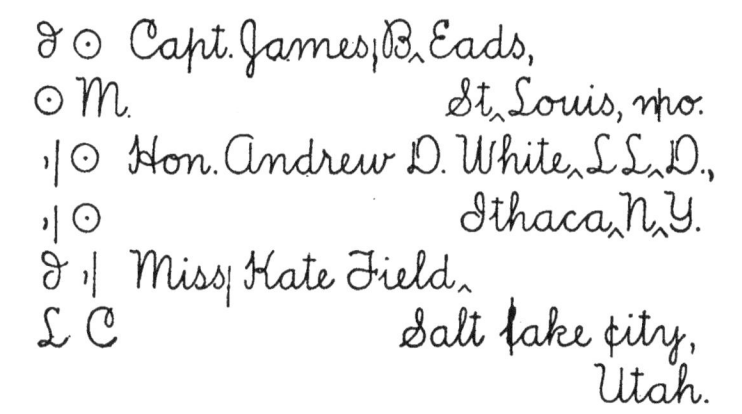

ꝺ ⊙   Capt. James₁B.∧Eads,
⊙ m.   St.∧Louis, mo.
,| ⊙   Hon. Andrew D. White∧L.∧L.∧D.,
,| ⊙   Ithaca∧N.∧Y.
ꝺ ,| Miss₁Kate Field∧
L C   Salt lake city,
              Utah.

C ,| Ocala, Marion ¢o., Fla.,
 ˅   Jan. 10, '99.
d| My Dear Friend,
                    Yours of the
  Si|o 2ᵗᵈ inst. was welcome.
  No ¶ (How I enjoyed the story
        of your Christmas vacation!
        You are an excellent letter-
     ¶ writer. [My vacation was spent
        quietly, but with "St. Nicholas",
        "The Youth's Companion", and
        "Nights with Uncle Remus" one
     tr could be/hardly dull.
                Very sincerely yours,
                  David Copperfield.
        Lemuel Gulliver,
          San Diego, Cal.

(margin: Joel Chandler Harris's)
(margin: Master)

REVIEW OF GRADED LESSONS.

WORDS — SPOKEN AND WRITTEN.

Spoken words are composed of **sounds**. Written words are composed of **letters** called (1) **vowels** — a, e, i, o, and u — representing the open sounds, and (2) **consonants** representing (*a*) obstructed breath vocalized; as, b, d, g, etc., called **sonants**, and (*b*) obstructed breath unvocalized; as, p, t, k, etc., called **surds**.

Spoken and written words form **verbal language**; and **tones**, **gestures**, and **facial expression** form **natural language** — used to reënforce spoken.

DEFINITION. — **English grammar** is the science which teaches the forms, uses, and relations of the words of the English language.

Language is used for the purpose of communicating thought, and the unit of thought, and of expression therefore, is

A SENTENCE.

DEFINITION. — A **sentence** is a group of words expressing a thought.

Its two parts are **subject** and **predicate**.

DEFINITIONS.

The **subject** of a sentence names that of which something is thought.

The **predicate** of a sentence tells what is thought.

A **phrase** is a group of words denoting related ideas but not expressing a thought.

A **clause** is a part of a sentence containing a subject and its predicate.

A **modifier** is a word or a group of words joined to some part of a sentence to qualify or limit the meaning.

The subject with its modifiers is called the **modified subject**; and the predicate with its modifiers is called the **modified predicate**.

Greece, which is the most noted country of antiquity, scarcely exceeded in size and in population the half of the state of New York.

The whole is a **sentence**; *Greece* is **subject**, *exceeded* is **predicate**; *Greece . . . antiquity* is the **modified subject**, *scarcely . . . New York* is the **modified predicate**; *which . . . antiquity* is a **clause**; *noted* and *scarcely* are **simple word modifiers**; *of antiquity* is a **simple phrase modifier**; *in size and in population* is a **compound phrase modifier**; *of the state of New York* is a **complex phrase modifier** — the phrase *of New York* modifying *state*, a word in the phrase *of the state* — and *which . . . antiquity* is a **clause modifier** of *Greece*.

DEFINITIONS.

The **analysis** of a sentence is the separation of it into its parts.

A **diagram** is a picture of the offices and relations of the different parts of a sentence.

Synthesis, construction, or **composition** is the putting together (1) of words, phrases, and clauses to form **sentences,** (2) of sentences to form a **paragraph,** and (3) of paragraphs to form a **theme.**

We group words into classes with respect to their office in the sentence. These classes, eight in number and called *parts of speech,* are the **noun,** the **pronoun,** the **verb,** the **adjective,** the **adverb,** the **preposition,** the **conjunction,** and the **interjection.**

The first five of these undergo what are called **modifications** — changes in form, meaning, and use.

CLAUSES CLASSIFIED.

He *that runs* may read it; He may read it *if he will keep the fact secret;* It is true *that he read it.*

In each of these sentences there are two clauses and two kinds of clauses. Those not italicized are **independent clauses;** those italicized are **dependent clauses** — the first an **adjective clause,** the second an **adverb clause** of condition, and the last a **noun clause explanatory.**

DEFINITIONS.

A **dependent clause** is one used as an adjective, an adverb, or a noun.

An **independent clause** is one not dependent on another clause.

SENTENCES CLASSIFIED.

Knowledge comes; Knowledge comes, but wisdom lingers; Knowledge comes, though wisdom lingers.

The first is a **simple sentence**; the second is a **compound sentence**, made up of two independent clauses; and the third is a **complex sentence**, made up of an independent and a dependent clause.

DEFINITIONS.

A **simple sentence** is one that contains but one subject and one predicate, either or both of which may be compound.

A **compound sentence** is one composed of two or more independent clauses.

A **complex sentence** is one composed of an independent clause and one or more dependent clauses.

John runs; Does John run? Run, John; How John runs!

The first sentence utters a fact, the second asks a question, the third issues a command, and the fourth expresses sudden feeling.

DEFINITIONS.

A **declarative sentence** is one that is used to affirm or to deny.

An **interrogative sentence** is one that expresses a question.

An **imperative sentence** is one that expresses a command or an entreaty.

An **exclamatory sentence** is one that expresses sudden thought or strong feeling.

THE NOUN.

Mary's mother, the *wife* of the *merchant*, bought her *daughter* a *house* a few *months* ago; My *son*, make wisdom the *object* of your life, for it is the principal *thing*.

The words italicized in these two sentences perform very different offices: (1) *mother* is **subject**, (2) *house* is **object**, (3) *Mary's* is a **possessive modifier** of *mother*, (4) *wife* is **explanatory** of *mother*, (5) *merchant* is **chief word** in a **prepositional phrase**, (6) *daughter* is **indirect object** of an action, (7) *months* has an **adverbial use measuring time**, (8) *son* is **independent** by address, (9) *object* is **objective complement**, and (10) *thing* is **attribute complement**. But, while discharging each a special function, they **all have one function**—they **name** persons or things, and hence are called **nouns**.

DEFINITION. — A noun is a name of anything.

There are two kinds of nouns — those naming all things of a certain class, and hence called **common nouns**, and those that are each the particular name of an individual of a class, and hence called **proper nouns**.

DEFINITIONS.

A **common noun** is a name which belongs to all things of a class.

A **proper noun** is the particular name of an individual.

Nouns have four **modifications** — number, gender, person, and **case**.

Number.

Definitions.

Number is that modification of a noun or pronoun which denotes one thing or more than one.

The **singular number** denotes one thing.

The **plural number** denotes more than one thing.

Rule. — The plural of nouns is regularly formed by adding **s** or **es** to the singular.

The **s** is a more common plural ending than the **es**.

The **es** is added (1) to words ending in **s, x, z, sh,** and **ch,** and makes a separate syllable, as in gases, foxes, topazes, lashes, and birches; (2) to many nouns in **o**, as in cargoes, negroes, and mottoes; (3) to nouns in **y,** the **y** when preceded by a consonant changing to **i**, as in cities, daisies, and skies; and (4) to some nouns in **f** or **fe**, the **f** or **fe** changing to **v**, as in loaves, calves, lives, and knives.

Some nouns form their plural **irregularly,** (1) by **internal change**, as in the six nouns, man, men; foot, feet; tooth, teeth; goose, geese; louse, lice; and mouse, mice; (2) by adding **en**, as in ox, oxen; child, children; and (3) by keeping the singular form, as in deer, deer; and sheep, sheep.

Gender.

Definitions.

Gender is that modification of a noun or pronoun which distinguishes sex.

The **masculine gender** denotes the male sex.

The **feminine gender** denotes the female sex.

The **neuter gender** denotes want of sex.

Gender in English follows the sex of the object named.

Strictly speaking, there can be but two genders, as there can be but two sexes — the names of objects without sex are of the **neuter** (neither) gender, therefore.

The three ways of distinguishing the feminine from the masculine are (1) by a **change of ending**, as in host, host**ess**; and Jew, Jew**ess**; (2) by a change of a word in the name, as in man-servant, **maid**-servant; gentleman, gentle**woman**; and peacock, pea**hen**; and (3) by the use of words wholly or radically different; as, boy, **girl**; lord, **lady**; and wizard, **witch**.

PERSON.

Number and gender are modifications of nouns affecting the meaning — number almost always indicated by the ending, gender sometimes.

Person is a modification of nouns that is not accompanied by form, as in

I Paul have written; *Paul*, thou art beside thyself; He brought *Paul* before Agrippa.

Paul retains its form, though in the first it names the speaker, and is of the **first** person; in the second it names the one spoken to, and is of the **second** person; and in the third it names the one spoken of, and is in the **third** person.

DEFINITIONS.

Person is that modification of a noun or pronoun which denotes the speaker, the one spoken to, or the one spoken of.

The **first person** denotes the one speaking.
The **second person** denotes the one spoken to.
The **third person** denotes the one spoken of.

CASE.

The *bear killed* the man; The *man killed* the *bear; Bear's grease* is made into hair oil.

In 1 the bear is represented as performing an action; in 2 as receiving an action; in 3 as possessing something. The word *bear* in these sentences has three different uses and is in the three cases — **nominative** in 1, **objective** in 2, and **possessive** in 3 — only the possessive being indicated by form.

In the illustrative sentences on p. 251, (1) the subject *mother*, *wife* explanatory of *mother*, *son* independent by address, and the attribute complement *thing* are all in the **nominative case**; (2) *Mary's*, possessive modifier of *mother*, is in the **possessive case**; and (3) *merchant*, principal word in a prepositional phrase, *daughter*, indirect object of an action, the object complement *house*, *months*, adverbial to denote measure, and *object*, the objective complement of *make*, are all in the **objective case**.

DEFINITIONS.

The **attribute complement** completes the predicate and belongs to the subject.

The **object complement** completes the predicate and names that which receives the act.

The **objective complement** completes the predicate and belongs to the object complement.

Case is that modification of a noun or pronoun which denotes its office in the sentence.

The **nominative case** of a noun or pronoun denotes its office as subject or as attribute complement.

The **possessive case** of a noun or pronoun denotes its office as possessive modifier.

The **objective case** of a noun or pronoun denotes its office as object complement, or as principal word in a prepositional phrase.

(The definitions of the nominative and objective cases give only their principal offices.)

DEFINITION. — **Declension** is the arrangement of the cases of nouns and pronouns in the two numbers.

DECLENSION OF NOUNS.

Nom. boy, boys, lady, ladies, man, men,
Pos. boy's, boys', lady's, ladies', man's, men's,
Obj. boy; boys. lady; ladies. man; men.

RULE. — The **possessive case** of nouns is formed in the singular by adding to the nominative the apostrophe and the letter **s** ('s); in the plural, by adding (') only. If the plural does not end in **s**, the apostrophe and the **s** are both added.

The preposition *of* and the objective may be used in place of the possessive — the wing *of the fly* = the *fly's* wing.

The possessive sign is added (1) to each of several nouns when modifying different words; as, Webster's and Worcester's dictionary; (2) to the last only, when modifying the same word; as, Ticknor & Field's bookstore.

THE PRONOUN.

Definition. — A pronoun is a word used for a noun. The word, phrase, or clause for which a pronoun stands is called its **antecedent**.

Pronouns have the modifications of nouns — **number, gender, person,** and **case**.

Classes.

Those that by their form denote the speaker, the one spoken to, and the one spoken of are called **personal pronouns** — *I*, of the first person; *thou* and *you*, of the second person; and *he*, *she*, and *it*, of the third person.

Those used in asking questions are called **interrogative pronouns** — *who*, *which*, and *what*.

Those that refer to some word or words in another clause and so connect clauses are called **relative pronouns** — *who*, *which*, *what*, and *that*.

Those used as adjectives and nouns — *all, some, both, many*, etc. — are called **adjective pronouns**.

Definitions.

A **personal pronoun** is one that by its form denotes the speaker, the one spoken to, or the one spoken of.

An **interrogative pronoun** is one with which a question is asked.

A **relative pronoun** is one that refers to some word or words in another clause and connects clauses.

An **adjective pronoun** is one that performs the offices of an adjective and a noun.

On pp. 186-188, we see (1) that personal, interrogative, and relative pronouns do not add **s** to form the plural; (2) that no personal pronoun, except *you*, forms its plural from the singular; (3) that no personal, interrogative, or relative pronoun has the apostrophe and **s** in the possessive singular or the apostrophe in the possessive plural; (4) that every personal pronoun has two forms in the possessive plural, and that all but *he* and *it* have two forms in the possessive singular; (5) that *he* is always masculine, *she* feminine, and *it* neuter, and that *I*, *you*, and *thou* are of any gender; (6) that *he*, *she*, and *it* have the same plural, and therefore *they*, *their*, and *them* are of any gender; (7) that *self* added to the possessives *my*, *thy*, and *your*, and to the objectives *him*, *her*, or *it*, makes our **compound personal pronouns** in the singular; (8) that *selves* added to *our* and *your* and to *them* makes the same pronouns in the plural; (9) that *who* and *which* have their plurals like the singular; (10) that *what* and *that* are indeclinable; (11) that *whose* is the possessive of the interrogative and the relative *who* and *which;* (12) that, excepting *that*, the relatives and the interrogatives are the same; (13) that *ever* and *soever* added to *who*, *which*, and *what* form our **compound relative pronouns**; (14) that the relative *who* represents persons; *which*, animals and things; *that*, persons, animals, and things; and *what*, things;

and (15) that the **only nominative** and **objective forms** in English — **eight** of one and **seven** of the other — are in the declensions of these three classes of pronouns.

Pronouns agree with their antecedents in number, gender, and case.

THE ADJECTIVE.

DEFINITION. — An **adjective** is a word used to modify a noun or a pronoun.

Good men; *six* marbles; *much* land; *this* book.

Good denotes quality; *six*, number; *much*, quantity; and *this*, the relation of the book to the speaker.

CLASSES OF ADJECTIVES.

DEFINITIONS.

A **descriptive adjective** is one that modifies by expressing quality.

A **definitive adjective** is one that modifies by pointing out, numbering, or denoting quantity.

In " A *wise, capable,* and *influential* teacher is *simple* and *unaffected* in speech and in bearing," we see that adjectives (1) may be **assumed**, and (2) may be **asserted** — standing in the predicate as **attribute complements**. We see (3) their **punctuation**, and (4) in **what order** they stand when of different length.

In "A *wise* man is respected," we may for the adjective *wise* substitute (5) the **equivalent phrase** *of wisdom* or (6) the **equivalent clause** *who is wise,* and thus secure **variety** of expression.

Care is needed in selecting apt adjectives, and in guarding against an **excessive** use of them.

COMPARISON.

Adjectives have one modification — **comparison** — seen in lovely, lovelier, loveliest; lovely, more lovely, most lovely; lovely, less lovely, least lovely. The terminations **er** and **est** and the prefixed adverbs **more** and **most** denote increase of the quality; the prefixed adverbs **less** and **least** denote **diminution.**

DEFINITIONS.

Comparison is a modification of the adjective to express the relative degree of the quality in the things compared.

The **positive degree** expresses the simple quality.

The **comparative degree** expresses a greater or a less degree of the quality.

The **superlative degree** expresses the greatest or the least degree of the quality.

If we suppose that in comparing we express increase oftener than decrease, and increase oftener by **er** and **est** than by **more** and **most**, we have the

RULE. — Adjectives are regularly compared by adding **er** to the positive to form the comparative, and **est** to the positive to form the superlative.

THE ADVERB.

DEFINITION. — An **adverb** is a word used to modify a verb, an adjective, or an adverb.

CLASSES OF ADVERBS.

Those that answer the question, *When?* are **adverbs of time**.

Those that answer the question, *Where?* are **adverbs of place**.

Those that answer the question, *To what extent?* are **adverbs of degree**.

Those that answer the question, *In what way?* are **adverbs of manner**.

Adverbs that connect clauses and modify words in them are called **conjunctive adverbs**.

In "We started *then*," we may substitute for the adverb *then* the phrase *at that time* or the clause *when the time came.*

Adverbs, then, may be expanded into equivalent phrases and clauses, and such phrases and clauses may be contracted into equivalent adverbs.

Adverbs, like adjectives, are compared. For the lists of adjectives and adverbs compared irregularly, see Lessons 87 and 88. In these lists it is seen that *more* and *most*, *less* and *least*, used in comparing adjectives and adverbs, are themselves comparatives and superlatives in er and est slightly disguised—see "Higher Lessons," Revised Edition, p. 259, foot-note.

Care is needed in the choice of adverbs, and in placing them and adverbial phrases where they belong.

THE VERB.

DEFINITION.—A **verb** is a word that asserts action, being, or state of being.

It **asserts**, whether the sentence affirms, denies, or questions.

CLASSES OF VERBS.

The boy *caught* a fish; Fish *swim*. *Caught* needs an object complement, as *fish*, to make a complete assertion; *swim* does not. *Caught* and all verbs that denote an act as going over from a doer to a receiver are **transitive**; *swim* and all verbs that do not require a word to complete the assertion are **intransitive**.

DEFINITIONS.

A **transitive** verb is one that requires an object.

An **intransitive** verb is one that does not require an object.

I *crush* the worm; I *crushed* the worm; The worm *crushed* by me died.

I *drive* the horses; I *drove* the horses; The horses *driven* by me ran away.

The past tense and the past participle *crushed* is formed by adding **ed** to the present *crush;* the past tense *drove* is formed by **vowel-change** of the present *drive;* and the past participle is formed by adding **en**. *Crush* and verbs like it are **regular**;[1] *drive* and those like it are **irregular**.[1]

DEFINITIONS.

A **regular verb** is one that forms its past tense and past participle by adding **ed** to the present.

An **irregular verb** is one that does not form its past tense and past participle by adding **ed** to the present.

---

[1] For another classification, see Lesson 74, foot-note.

Verbs have the modifications called **voice, mode, tense, number,** and **person.**

VOICE.

I *drove* the horses; The horses *were driven* by me.

Drove shows that the subject denotes the actor; *were driven* shows that the subject names the ones acted upon. These uses of the verb constitute the modification called **voice**: *drove* is in the **active** voice, and *were driven* is in the **passive**.

DEFINITIONS.

Voice is that modification of the transitive verb which shows whether the subject names the actor or the thing acted upon.

The **active voice** shows that the subject names the actor.

The **passive voice** shows that the subject names the thing acted upon.

MODE.

James *walks;* James *may walk;* If James *walk* out, he wil! improve; James, *walk* on.

Here the action is asserted (1) as a fact, (2) as possible, (3) as conceivable, and (4) as a command; and these ways of asserting give us the four modes — **indicative, potential, subjunctive,** and **imperative.** Lesson 90, foot-note.

DEFINITIONS.

Mode is that modification of the verb which denotes the manner of asserting the action or being.

The **indicative mode** asserts the action or being as a fact.

The **potential mode** asserts the power, liberty, possibility, or necessity of acting or being.

The **subjunctive mode** asserts the action or being as a mere supposition, conception, or wish.

The **imperative mode** asserts the action or being as a command or an entreaty.

TENSE.

I *walk;* I *walked;* I *shall walk;* I *have walked;* I *had walked;* I *shall have walked.*

In the first three sentences, the action is asserted as **taking place** in time (1) present, (2) past, and (3) future; in the last three it is asserted as finished or **completed** in time (4) present, (5) past, and (6) future.

DEFINITIONS.

Tense is that modification of the verb which expresses the time of the action or being.

The **present tense** expresses action or being as present.

The **past tense** expresses action or being as past.

The **future tense** expresses action or being as yet to come.

The **present perfect tense** expresses action or being as completed at the present time.

The **past perfect tense** expresses action or being as completed at some past time.

The **future perfect tense** expresses action or being to be completed at some future time.

PERSON AND NUMBER.

I walk; Thou walk**est**; He walk**s**; They walk. *Walk* adds the ending **est** and **s** in the second and third sentences to make the verb agree in person with the subjects *thou* and *he;* adds **s** in the third sentence and omits it in the first and the fourth to make the verb agree in number with its subjects *he, I,* and *they.*

DEFINITION.—**Number** and **person** of a verb are those modifications that show its agreement with the number and person of its subject.

The **infinitive** and the **participle** are forms of the verb that do not assert.

The infinitive is ordinarily found with the preposition *to*, and forms with it the **infinitive phrase**—used as an **adjective**, an **adverb**, or a **noun**.

The participle has an adjective or a noun[1] nature plus its constant verb nature.

DEFINITIONS.

The **infinitive** is a form of the verb which names the action or being in a general way, without asserting it of anything.

The **participle** is a form of the verb partaking of the nature of an adjective or of a noun,[1] and expressing the action or being as assumed.

The **present participle** denotes action or being as continuing at the time indicated by the predicate.

The **past participle** denotes action or being as past or completed at the time indicated by the predicate.

---

[1] When it has a noun nature it may be called a **nounal verb.** See Lesson 98.

The **past perfect participle** denotes action or being as completed at a time previous to that indicated by the predicate.

Conjugation is the regular arrangement of all the forms of the verb.

Synopsis is the regular arrangement of the forms of one number and person in all the modes and tenses.

The **principal parts** of a verb are the present indicative or infinitive, the past indicative, and the past participle.

Auxiliary verbs are those that help in the conjugation of other verbs.

The auxiliaries are *do, be, have, shall, will, may, can,* and *must.*

Defective verbs are those verbs some of whose parts are wanting — *can, may, must, ought, shall,* and *will.*

For the Review of the **conjugation** of verbs — **simple** form, **emphatic** form, **progressive** form, and **passive** form — see Lessons 92, 93, and 94.

THE PREPOSITION.

DEFINITION. — A **preposition** is a word that introduces a phrase modifier, and shows the relation, in sense, of its principal word to the word modified.

Such phrase modifiers have the force of adjectives or adverbs. Care is needed in choosing the right preposition, and in placing the prepositional phrase where it belongs.

THE CONJUNCTION.

DEFINITION.—A **conjunction** is a word used to connect words, phrases, or clauses.

Relative pronouns and conjunctive adverbs and prepositions also connect, but the conjunction is the only part of speech which simply connects.

DEFINITIONS.

Coördinate conjunctions are such as connect words, phrases, or clauses of the same rank.

Subordinate conjunctions are such as connect clauses of different rank.

THE INTERJECTION.

DEFINITION.—An **interjection** is a word used to express strong or sudden feeling.

Interjections are without grammatical relation to any word in the sentence.

For a Review of the **paragraph**, of paragraphs forming a **theme**; of general **topic, sub-topic, framework, matter,** and **style**; and of **descriptive, narrative,** and **persuasive** writing, see Lessons 30, 40, 50, 60, 70, and 77.

For a Summary of the **rules for capital letters** and **punctuation**, and for illustrative examples, see pp. 224–229.

For **letter-writing** under **heading, introduction, body of the letter, conclusion, folding,** and **superscription,** see pp. 229–243.

For a Summary of the **rules of syntax**, see p. 244.

For the ordinary **proof-marks**, see pp. 245, 246.

For **schemes for review**, see pp. 267–270.

For **abbreviations**, see pp. 272–277.

SCHEMES FOR REVIEW.

These Schemes will be found very helpful in a general review. The pupils should be able to reproduce them, omitting the Lesson numbers.

SCHEME FOR THE SENTENCE.

(*The numbers refer to Lessons.*)

PARTS.
- Subject.
  - Noun or Pronoun (6, 14, 19).
  - Phrase (49).
  - Clause (61).
- Predicate. Verb (6, 16).
- Complements.
  - Object.
    - Noun or Pronoun (39).
    - Phrase (49).
    - Clause (61).
  - Attribute.
    - Adjective (39).
    - Noun or Pronoun (42).
    - Phrase (49).
    - Clause (61).
- Modifiers.
  - Adjectives (20, 22).
  - Adverbs (24, 27).
  - Participles (48).
  - Nouns and Pronouns (53).
  - Phrases (31, 48, 49).
  - Clauses (57, 59).
- Connectives.
  - Conjunctions (35, 36, 62).
  - Pronouns (57).
  - Adverbs (59).
- Independent Parts (36, 64).

Classes — Meaning. — Declarative, Interrogative, Imperative, Exclamatory (63).

Classes — Form. — Simple, Complex, Compound (57, 62).

SCHEME FOR THE NOUN.

(*The numbers refer to Lessons.*)

NOUN (14).
- **Uses.**
  - Subject (6).
  - Object Complement (39).
  - Objective Complement (82).
  - Attribute Complement (42).
  - Adjective Modifier (53).
  - Prin. word in Prep. Phrase (34).
  - Independent (64).
- **Classes.**
  - Common (71).
  - Proper (71).
- **Modifications.**
  - Number. { Singular (78, 79). / Plural (78, 79). }
  - Gender. { Masculine / Feminine / Neuter } (80).
  - Person. { First / Second / Third } (81–83).
  - Case. { Nominative / Possessive / Objective } (81–85).

SCHEME FOR THE PRONOUN.

PRONOUNS.
- **Uses.** — Same as those of the Noun.
- **Classes.** { Personal / Relative / Interrogative / Adjective } (71, 72).
- **Modifications.** — Same as those of the Noun.

SCHEME FOR THE VERB.

(The numbers refer to Lessons.)

VERB.
- **Uses.**
  - To assert action, being, or state — Predicate (6, 16).
  - To assume action, being, or state. { Participles (48). / Infinitives (49). }
- **Classes.**
  - Form. { Regular (74). / Irregular (74, 91). }
  - Meaning. { Transitive (74). / Intransitive (74). }
- **Modifications.**
  - Voice. { Active (89). / Passive (89). }
  - Mode. { Indicative / Potential / Subjunctive / Imperative } (90–94).
  - Tense. { Present / Past / Future / Present Perfect / Past Perfect / Future Perfect } (90–94).
  - Number. { Singular / Plural } (90, 92–95).
  - Person. { First / Second / Third } (90, 92–95).
- **Participles.** — Classes. { Present / Past / Past Perfect } (90–94, 96, 98).
- **Infinitives.** — Tenses. { Present / Present Perfect } (90, 92–94).

SCHEME FOR THE ADJECTIVE.

(The numbers refer to Lessons.)

ADJECTIVE.
- Uses.
  - Modifier (20, 22).
  - Attribute Complement (39).
- Classes.
  - Descriptive (73).
  - Definitive (73).
- Modification. — Comparison.
  - Pos. Deg.
  - Comp. "
  - Sup. "
  (87, 88).

SCHEME FOR THE ADVERB.

ADVERB.
- Classes.
  - Time
  - Place
  - Degree
  - Manner
  (75).
- Modification. — Comparison.
  - Pos. Deg.
  - Comp. "
  - Sup. "
  (87, 88).

SCHEME FOR THE CONJ., PREP., AND INT.

THE CONJUNCTION. — Classes.
- Coördinate
- Subordinate
(36, 76). No Modifications.

THE PREPOSITION (34, 41). — No Classes. No Modifications.

THE INTERJECTION (36). — No Classes. No Modifications.

Model for Written Parsing adapted to all Parts of Speech. — *Oh! it has a voice for those who on their sick beds lie and waste away.*

Sentence.	CLASSIFICATION.		MODIFICATIONS.							SYNTAX.
	Class.	Sub-class.	Voice.	Mode.	Tense.	Per.	Num.	Gen.	Case.	Deg. of Comp.	
Oh!	Int.										Independent.
it	Pro.	Per.		Ind.	Pres.	3d.	Sing.	Neut.	Nom.		Sub. of *has*.
has	Vb.	Ir., Tr.	Act.	Ind.	Pres.	3d.	Sing.	Neut.	Nom.		Pred. of *it*.
a	Adj.	Def.									Mod. of *voice*.
voice	N.	Com.				"	"	"	Obj.		Obj. Com. of *has*.
for	Prep.										Shows relation of *has* to *those*.
those	Pro.	Adj.					Plu.	M. or F.	"		Prin. word after *for*.
who	Pro.	Rel.				"	"	"	Nom.		Sub. of *lie* and *waste*.
on	Prep.										Shows relation of *lie* to *beds*.
their	Pro.	Per.				"	"	"	Pos.	Pos.	Poss. Mod: of *beds*.
sick	Adj.	Des.									Mod. of *beds*.
beds	N.	Com.				"	"	Neut.	Obj.		Prin. word after *on*.
lie	Vb.	Ir., Int.		Ind.	Pres.	"	"				Pred. of *who*.
and	Conj.	Coör.									Con. *lie* and *waste*.
waste	Vb.	Reg., Int.		"	"	"	"				Pred. of *who*.
away	Adv.	Place									Mod. of *waste*.

For exercises in general parsing, select from the preceding Lessons on Analysis.

ABBREVIATIONS.

Remarks. — Few abbreviations are allowable in ordinary composition. They are very convenient in writing lists of articles, in scientific works, and wherever certain terms occur frequently.

Titles prefixed to proper names are generally abbreviated, except in addressing an officer of high rank. Titles that immediately follow names are almost always abbreviated.

Names of women are not generally abbreviated, except by using an initial for one of two Christian names.

Abbreviations that shorten only by one letter are unnecessary; as, *Jul.* for "July," *Jno.* for "John," *da.* for "day," etc.

1*st*, 2*d*, 3*d*, 4*th*, etc. are not followed by the period. They are not treated as abbreviations.

@, At.
A.B. or B.A. (*Artium Baccalaureus*), Bachelor of Arts.
Acct., acct., or %, Account.
A.D., (*Anno Domini*), In the year of our Lord.
Adjt., Adjutant.
Æt. or æt. (*ætatis*), Of age, aged.
Ala., Alabama.
Alex., Alexander.
A.M. or M.A. (*Artium Magister*), Master of Arts.
A.M. or a.m. (*ante meridiem*), Before noon.
Amt., Amount.
And., Andrew.

Anon., Anonymous.
Ans., Answer.
Anth., Anthony.
Apr., April.
Arch., Archibald.
Ark., Arkansas.
Ariz., Arizona.
Atty., Attorney.
Atty.-Gen., Attorney-General.
Aug., August; Augustus.
Av. or Ave., Avenue.
Avoir., Avoirdupois.
Bart., Baronet.
bbl., Barrels.
B.C., Before Christ.
Benj., Benjamin.
Brig.-Gen., Brigadier-General.

Abbreviations.

B.S., Bachelor of Science.
bu., Bushel.
¢ or ct., Cents.
Cal., California.
Cap., Capital.   Caps., Capitals.
Capt., Captain.
C.E., Civil Engineer.
cf. (*confer*), Compare.
Chas., Charles.
Chron., Chronicles.
Co., Company; County.
c/o, In care of.
C.O.D., Collect on delivery.
Col., Colonel; Colossians.
Coll., College; Collector.
Conn., Connecticut.
Cor., Corinthians.
Cr., Credit; Creditor.
cub. ft., Cubic feet.
cub. in., Cubic inches.
cwt., Hundredweight.
d., Days; Pence.
Danl. or Dan., Daniel.
D.C., District of Columbia.
D.C.L., Doctor of Civil Law.
D.D. (*Divinitatis Doctor*), Doctor of Divinity.
D.D.S., Doctor of Dental Surgery.
Dec., December.
Del., Delaware.

Deut., Deuteronomy.
D.G. (*Dei gratia*), By the grace of God.
Dist.-Atty., District-Attorney.
D.M., Doctor of Music.
do. (*ditto*), The same.
doz., Dozen.
Dr., Doctor; Debtor.
D.V. (*Deo volente*), God willing.
E., East.
Eben., Ebenezer.
Eccl., Ecclesiastes.
Ed., Edition; Editor.
Edm., Edmund.
Edw., Edward.
e.g. (*exempli gratia*), For example.
E.N.E., East-northeast.
Eng., English; England.
Eph., Ephesians; Ephraim.
E.S.E., East-southeast.
Esq., Esquire.
et al. (*et alibi*), And elsewhere.
et al. (*et alii*), And others.
et seq. (*et sequentia*), And following.
etc. or &c. (*et cœtera*), And others; And so forth.
Ex., Example; Exodus.
Ez., Ezra.

Ezek., Ezekiel.
Fahr. or F., Fahrenheit (thermometer).
Feb., February.
Fla., Florida.
Fr., French; France.
Fran., Francis.
Fred., Frederic.
Fri., Friday.
ft., Feet.
Ft., Fort.
fur., Furlong.
Ga., Georgia.
Gal., Galatians.
gal., Gallons.
Gen., General; Genesis.
Geo., George.
Gov., Governor.
gr., Grains.
h., Hours.
Hab., Habakkuk.
Hag., Haggai.
H.B.M., His (or Her) Britannic Majesty.
hdkf., Handkerchief.
Heb., Hebrews.
H.H., His Holiness (the Pope).
hhd., Hogsheads.
H.M., His (or Her) Majesty.
Hon., Honorable.
Hos., Hosea.

H.R.H., His (or Her) Royal Highness.
ib. or ibid (*ibidem*), In the same place.
id. (*idem*), The same.
i e. (*id est*), That is.
I.H.S. (*Jesus hominum Salvator*), Jesus the Savior of Men.
Ill., Illinois.
in., Inches.
incog. (*incognito*), Unknown.
Ind., Indiana.
Ind. T., Indian Territory.
inst., Instant, the present month.
Io., Iowa.
I.O.O.F., Independent Order of Odd Fellows.
Isa., Isaiah.
Jac., Jacob.
Jan., January.
Jas., James.
Jer., Jeremiah.
Jona., Jonathan.
Jos., Joseph.
Josh., Joshua.
Jr. or Jun., Junior.
Judg., Judges.
Kans. or Kan., Kansas.
Ky., Kentucky.
L., Latin.
l, Line; ll., Lines.

£ or **£**, Pounds sterling.
La., Louisiana.
Lam., Lamentations.
lb. or **℔.** (*libra* or *libræ*), Pound or pounds in weight.
l.c., Lower case (small letter).
Lev., Leviticus.
L.I., Long Island.
Lieut., Lieutenant.
LL.B. (*Legum Baccalaureus*), Bachelor of Laws.
LL.D. (*Legum Doctor*), Doctor of Laws.
M. or **Mons.**, Monsieur.
M. (*meridies*), Noon.
m., Miles; Minutes.
Mad., Madam. **Mme.**, Madame.
Maj., Major.
Mal., Malachi.
Mar., March.
Mass., Massachusetts.
Matt., Matthew.
M.C., Member of Congress.
M.D. (*Medicinæ Doctor*), Doctor of Medicine.
Md., Maryland.
mdse., Merchandise.
Me., Maine.
Mem., Memorandum; Memoranda.
Messrs., Messieurs.
Mgr., Monseigneur.

Mic., Micah.
Mich., Michigan; Michael.
Minn., Minnesota.
Miss., Mississippi.
Mlle., Mademoiselle.
Mmes., Mesdames.
Mo., Missouri.
mo., Months.
Mon., Monday.
M.P., Member of Parliament.
Mont., Montana.
Mr., Mister.
Mrs., Mistress (pronounced Missis).
MS., Manuscript.
MSS., Manuscripts.
Mt., Mountain.
N., North.
N.A., North America.
Nath., Nathaniel.
N.B. (*nota bene*), Mark well.
N.C., North Carolina.
N.Dak., North Dakota.
N.E., New England.
N.E., Northeast.
Neh., Nehemiah.
Neth., Netherlands.
Nev., Nevada.
N.H., New Hampshire.
N.J., New Jersey.
N.Mex. or **N.M.**, New Mexico.
N.N.E., North-northeast.

N.N.W., North-northwest.
N.O., New Orleans.
No. (*numero*), Number.
Nov., November.
N.W., Northwest.
N.Y., New York.
O., Ohio.
Obad., Obadiah.
Oct., October.
Oreg. or Or., Oregon.
Oxon. (*Oxonia*), Oxford.
oz., Ounces.
p., Page. pp., Pages.
Pa. or Penn., Pennsylvania.
Payt. or payt., Payment.
per cent or per ct. or % (*per centum*), By the hundred.
Ph.D. (*Philosophiæ Doctor*), Doctor of Philosophy.
Phil., Philip; Philippians.
Phila., Philadelphia.
pk., Pecks.
P.M., Postmaster.
P.M. or p.m. (*post meridiem*), Afternoon.
P.O., Post Office.
Pres., President.
Prof., Professor.
Pro tem. (*pro tempore*), For the time being.
Prov., Proverbs.

prox. (*proximo*), The next month.
P.S., Postscript.
Ps., Psalms.
pt., Pints.
pwt., Pennyweights.
qt., Quarts.
q.v. (*quod vide*), Which see.
Qy., Query.
rd., Rods.
Recd., Received.
Rev., Reverend; Revelation.
R.I., Rhode Island.
Robt., Robert.
Rom., Romans (Book of); Roman letters.
R.R., Railroad.
R.S.V.P. (*Répondez s'il vous plait*), Answer, if you please.
Rt. Hon., Right Honorable.
Rt. Rev., Right Reverend.
S., South.
s., Shillings.
S.A., South America.
Saml. or Sam., Samuel.
Sat., Saturday.
S.C., South Carolina.
S. Dak., South Dakota.
S.E., Southeast.
Sec., Secretary.
sec., seconds.

Sep. or Sept., September.
Sol., Solomon.
sq. ft., Square feet.
sq. in., Square inches.
sq. m., Square miles.
S.S.E., South-southeast.
S.S.W., South-southwest.
St., Street; Saint.
Sun., Sunday.
Supt., Superintendent.
S.W., Southwest.
T., Tons; Tuns.
Tenn., Tennessee.
Tex., Texas.
Theo., Theodore.
Theoph., Theophilus.
Thess., Thessalonians.
Thos., Thomas.
Thurs., Thursday.
Tim., Timothy.
tr., Transpose.
Treas., Treasurer.
Tues., Tuesday.
ult. (*ultimo*), Last — last month.
U.S. or U.S.A., United States of America; United States Army.
U.S.M., United States Mail.
U.S.N., United States Navy.
Va., Virginia.
Vice-Pres., Vice-President.
viz. (*videlicet*), To wit, namely.
vol., Volume.
vs. (*versus*), Against.
Vt., Vermont.
W., West.
Wed., Wednesday.
w.f., Wrong font.
Wis., Wisconsin.
wk., Weeks.
Wm., William.
W.N.W., West-northwest.
W.S.W., West-southwest.
W. Va., West Virginia.
Wyo., Wyoming.
Xmas, Christmas.
yd., Yards.
y. or yr., Years.
Zech., Zechariah.
& Co., And Company.

INDEX.

	PAGE
Abbreviations	77, 78, 272-277
Adjectives,	
abuse of	43, 44
an and *a*	42
arrangement of	52, 53
choice of	41-44, 54, 55
classes of	161, 162
comparison of	192-196
definition of	39, 161
distinguished from adverbs.	83, 84
effect upon style	41
"scheme" for review	270
Adverbs,	
arrangement of	82-84, 118
classes of	166
comparison of	194-196
conjunctive	167, 169, 170
definition of	49
distinguished from adjectives	83, 84
"scheme" for review	270
use of	48-52
Agreement	18, 22, 74-76
Analysis, oral	26, 31, 35, 45, 47, 49, 63, 68, 71, 73, 82, 104, 106, 116, 126, 130, 137, 140
Antecedent	160
Argument	123
Arrangement	90-94
Articles	88, 42
Auxiliary Verbs	201
Be	209-212
Capital Letters, rules.	19, 27, 31, 77, 162, 224, 225
Clauses,	
arrangement of	180-182
definition of	125
dependent, { adjective	124-128
{ adverb	129-132
{ noun	136-139
independent	125, 140, 141

	PAGE
Colon	139, 227
Comma	76, 77, 118, 127, 226
Complements, { attribute	80, 81, 95, 112
{ object	80, 81
{ objective	183, 184
Composition	18
Conjugation	201
Conjunctions, { classes of	167
{ definition of	72, 166
Connectives, list of	169, 170
Contraction	148-151
Diagrams, { definition	17
{ use of	5, 6
Expansion	148-151
Exposition	145, 146
Figurative Expressions	154
Framework	89, 118, 124
Grammar, English	12
Indirect Object	185
Infinitive Phrase	105-107
Interjections	72, 73
Interrogation Point	142, 225
Knowledge, { first hand	59, 60
{ second hand	59, 60
Language, { natural	12
{ talk on	9-14
{ verbal	12
Letters, { consonants, { sonants	11, 12
{ { surds	11, 12
{ vowels	11, 12
{ what	9-12
Letter-Writing	229-243
Modifications	176, 177

279

Graded Lessons in English.

	PAGE
a	84
adjective	88–44
Modifier, adverb	44–52
clause	118, 119, 124, 182
noun	115, 116, 118
phrase	61–69, 118, 119
Modified Predicate	44, 45
Modified Subject	83, 84
Negatives	94
Nominative Forms	190
Notional Verb	219 (note)
classes of	157, 158
declension of	185
definition of	25, 26
Nouns, modifications of { case	182, 185, 188–190
gender	178, 179
number	74, 75, 175–178
person	180–182
modifiers, as	115, 116, 185
"scheme" for review	269
ten offices of	251
Object	164 (note)
Objective Forms	190
Objects writers have	153, 154
Order, usual and transposed	69, 90–94
composition of	55–60, 87, 89, 108–113, 155, 156, 173, 174
definition of	55, 56, 58, 156
framework for	89, 113, 124
Paragraphs, kinds of, illustrated, { descriptive	108–113, 171–173
explanatory	56–60
narrative	85–89, 133–135
persuasive	133–135, 152–154
length of	124
material for	59, 60
order of	89, 173
relation of	58, 59, 88, 89
topics and sub-topics of	89, 124
Parsing	26, 29, 81, 89, 73, 106, 130, 192, 218, 271

	PAGE
Participle	102–105
Parts of Speech	25
Period	19, 77, 225
arrangement	76, 77, 90–94
change of	66, 67
complex	101
compound	101
definition	62
Phrases, discussion of	60–62
infinitive	105–107
participial	107, 108
position of	90, 92
prepositional	60–64
transposed	90, 91
Possessive Forms	188–190
Predicate	15–24, 27–29, 86, 44, 45, 70, 79, 81
Prepositions	67, 68, 94
agreement of	76, 191
classes of	158, 159, 187, 188
declension of	186–188
definition of	81, 159
discussion of	80–82
Pronouns, modifications of { case	180–185, 190
gender	178, 179
number	187–189
person	180–185
modifiers, as	115–117, 184
"scheme" for review	268
Proof-Marks	245, 246
colon	189, 227
comma	76, 77, 118, 127, 226
exclamation point	78, 225
(explanation of restrictive)	118, 119
Punctuation, interrogation point	142, 225
Rules for, period	19, 77, 225
quotation marks	135, 188, 139
semicolon	184, 158, 227
summary of rules for all points	225–229
Quotations, { direct	188, 139
indirect	188, 139

Index. 281

Review of Graded Lessons,
- adjectives 258, 259
- adverbs 259, 260
- conjunctions 266
- interjections 266
- nouns 251-255
- prepositions 265
- pronouns 256-258
- sentences 247-251
- verbs 260-265

Review Questions ...15, 21, 27, 36, 37, 47, 48, 55, 71, 84, 108, 132, 183, 150-152, 170, 171, 179, 180, 191, 195, 196, 218

See 203-205

S-Ending 18-20, 22, 32, 36, 74, 75, 120

Sentences,
- analysis of 16, 17
- definition of 14
- diagram of 16, 17
- parts of 15
- predicate of 16, 21, 29, 45, 70, 79-82
- study of 3-5
- subject of 16, 17, 26, 70

Sentences (classes),
- form,
  - complex 126-132
  - compound 140, 141
  - simple 126
- meaning,
  - declarative 141, 142
  - exclamatory 141, 142
  - imperative 141, 142
  - interrogative . 24, 141, 142

Sounds 9-12

Subject .. 15-24, 26, 32, 35, 70, 106, 107, 136, 137

Synopsis 201

Syntax, rules of 244
Synthesis 18
Theme 124
To, with infinitive 105, 106, 118

Verbs,
- agreement of ...17-20, 22, 32, 36, 74-76, 213-215
- classes,
  - intransitive . 162-164
  - irregular ...164, 165, 201, 202
  - regular 163-165
  - strong .... 164 (note)
  - transitive ... 162-164
  - weak ..... 164 (note)
- classified
  - form 163-165
  - meaning 162-164
- conjugation of 201-212
- definition of 28
- emphatic form 206
- infinitive, the 105, 200
- modifications of
  - mode 198-200
  - number 199, 200
  - person 199, 200
  - tense 198, 200
  - voice 196, 197
- participle .... 102-105, 200, 219 (note), 220
- participle distinguished from predicate 215-218
- passive form 212
- principal parts 201
- progressive form 213
- "scheme" for review 269

What 160